The Psychology Student
Writer's Manual

SECOND EDITION

The Psychology Student Writer's Manual

Jill M. Scott
University of Central Oklahoma

Russell E. Koch
University of Oklahoma

Gregory M. Scott
University of Central Oklahoma

Stephen M. Garrison
University of Central Oklahoma

Prentice Hall

Upper Saddle River, New Jersey 07458

Library of Congress Cataloging-in-Publication Data

The psychology student writer's manual / Jill M. Scott ... [et al.].—2nd ed.
    p. cm.
  Includes bibliographical references (p.) and index.
  ISBN 0-13-041382-8
    1. Psychology—Authorship—Handbooks, manuals, etc.   2. Psychological
  literature—Authorship—Handbooks, manuals, etc.   3. Report writing—Handbooks,
  manuals, etc.   I. Scott, Jill Mackay

  BF76.8 .P76 2002
  808'.06615—dc21

2001 018536

VP, Editorial Director: Laura Pearson
Acquisitions Editor: Jayme Heffler
Editorial Assistant: April Dawn Klemm
Managing Editor: Mary Rottino
Production Liaison: Fran Russello
Editorial/Production Supervision: Marianne Hutchinson (Pine Tree Composition, Inc.)
Prepress and Manufacturing Buyer: Tricia Kenny
Art Director: Jayne Conte
Cover Designer: Bruce Kenselaar
Senior Marketing Manager: Sharon Cosgrove

This book was set in 10/12 Baskerville by Pine Tree Composition, Inc.,
and was printed and bound by R.R. Donnelley & Sons Company.
The cover was printed by Phoenix Color Corp.

©2002, 1999 by Pearson Education, Inc.
Upper Saddle River, New Jersey 07458

Printed in the United States of America
10 9 8 7 6 5 4 3 2

ISBN 0-13-041382-8

Prentice-Hall International (UK) Limited, *London*
Prentice-Hall of Australia Pty. Limited, *Sydney*
Prentice-Hall Canada Inc., *Toronto*
Prentice-Hall Hispanoamericana, S. A., *Mexico*
Prentice-Hall of India Private Limited, *New Delhi*
Prentice-Hall of Japan, Inc., *Tokyo*
Pearson Education Asia Pte. Ltd, *Singapore*
Editora Prentice-Hall do Brasil, Ltda., *Rio de Janeiro*

To
Andrew and Nicole

Contents

To the Student

This second edition of *The Psychology Student Writer's Manual* contains new information that will help you stay current in the constantly changing worlds of psychology and information technology. Regardless of the continuing stream of new insights that psychological research produces, however, some things remain the same. Successful students, like successful psychologists, for example, will always be competent writers. As students of psychology we observe human behavior. In psychological research we write for three purposes: (1) to record what we observe, (2) to explain what we record, and (3) to defend what we explain. As psychologists we write to contribute to the efforts of other disciplines like sociology, economics, and anthropology, to understand who we are as human beings.

Writing is fundamental not only to communicating, but also to learning itself. When you try to communicate your ideas to others by writing them down, you are faced with the task of refining and clarifying your thoughts, and therefore you learn more about the subject you are writing about than you would otherwise. *The Psychology Writer's Manual,* therefore, is designed to help you improve your writing and learn psychology. These two objectives are addressed in the three major sections of this book.

The Introduction tells you what psychology is all about. Intended for both first-time and experienced psychology students, the Introduction offers a basic historical orientation and a brief overview of the scope of issues currently addressed by psychologists.

Part One of the book addresses fundamental concerns of all writers, exploring the reasons why we write, describing the writing process itself, and examining those elements of grammar, style, and punctuation that cause the most confusion among writers in general. A vital concern throughout this part, and the rest of the book as well, is the three-way interrelationship among writer, topic, and audience. Our discussion of this relationship aims at building your self-confidence as you clarify your goals. Writing is not a magical process beyond the control of most people. It is instead a series of interconnected skills that any writer can improve with practice, and the end result of this practice is power. Part One of this manual treats the act of writing not as an empty exercise undertaken only to produce a grade but as a powerful learning tool, as well as the primary medium by which psychologists accomplish their goals. Chapter 3 explains the importance of formatting the research paper properly and supplies you with format models for title pages, tables of contents, and so on. Chapter 4 explains how to cite sources and discusses the crucial responsibility of every psychology writer to use source material ethically.

Part Two of this manual is new revised in this second edition. Chapter 5 tells you how to organize your writing process and Chapter 6 introduces you to the fundamentals of library research. Chapter 7 is almost entirely new. It provides a list of internet sites that lead to many other sites that tell you many things you need to know about both writing and psychology. For those of you who are taking or considering taking distance learning courses, this chapter introduces you to the special challenges and opportunities of distance learning.

Each chapter in Part Three explains how to write a paper commonly assigned in psychology courses everywhere. Some assignments are for introductory students and others are for advanced courses.

Your professor may give you a specific paper assignment from one of these chapters. If your professor does not make your assignment specific, you may want to select an assignment and discuss your selection with your instructor before proceeding. We wish you all success as you accept a primary challenge of academic and professional life: to write, and write well.

Jill Scott, Russ Koch, Greg Scott, and Steve Garrison

To the Teacher

This book has been updated and improved to help you deal with two problems commonly faced by teachers of psychology. First, students often need substantial specific direction to produce a good paper. How many times have you assigned papers in your psychology classes and found yourself teaching the class how to write the paper—not only content, but form and grammar as well? This text, which may accompany the primary text you assign in any psychology class or stand on its own, allows you to assign one of the papers explained in Part Three with the knowledge that virtually everything the student needs to know, from grammar to sources of information to citing sources, is here within one book. In addition to many updated examples throughout the text, the second edition features a substantially revised Chapter 7: The Internet and Distance Learning. This chapter helps distance learners to understand the special problems and opportunities of distance learning while providing them with selected internet sites that will lead them to a vast amount of information on both writing and psychology.

This manual provides you with options for paper assignments for both beginning and advanced students. Your introductory courses, for example, might feature assignments from Chapter 8, in which students apply their creative writing efforts to understanding extrasensory perception, sensation, or child development. Students in your advanced courses will find the explicit directions in chapters ten through thirteen most helpful. If you are teaching a distance learning course, this manual is particularly helpful. You may, for example, direct your students to "Conduct a literature review as described in Chapter 9, following directions for format and style provided in Part One of the text."

As you know, writing skill is essential not only to becoming an effective student, but to succeeding professionally as well. This book is written to assist you in leading students toward that success. In addition, a major problem faced by teachers who require written assignments is plagiarism. Although only the most exceptional diligence will eliminate plagiarism entirely, this book will help you to take one of the most effective preventative actions. In an age when whole papers can be downloaded from the Internet, one of the best ways to ensure an original paper is to make your assignment directions very specific. If your direction to students is "Write something on memory," it is relatively easy for a student to find a paper already prepared. If, on the other hand, you provide a very specific list of instructions, such as those in the chapters in this book, students who might otherwise be tempted to submit work that is not their own will find that it does not meet the requirements of the assignment.

We wish you the best in your endeavors and welcome your comments.

Jill Scott, Russ Koch, Greg Scott, and Steve Garrison
Edmond and Norman, Oklahoma

Introduction: The Discipline of Psychology

Is psychology new to you?

If you are about to write your first paper in psychology, this introduction is for you. It will help you understand what psychology is and what psychologists are trying to achieve when they write, knowledge that will save you time and effort. You may want to read other books about psychology before you begin to write, but some of the most important information you will need is right here, in a brief overview of the discipline.

Are you an experienced student of psychology who needs to review trends in the discipline?

If you have already studied psychology in some detail, you may want to skip this introduction and read Chapters 1 through 7, which discuss writing and research in general, and then the particular chapter in Part Three that provides the directions for the specific type of paper you have been assigned. You may find, however, that the introduction helps to refresh your memory and establish your current writing efforts more firmly within the broader framework of the discipline. Wherever you may be in your progress toward mastering the methods and contributing to the rich tradition of psychology, you are encouraged to read this section.

A Brief History

Our modern concepts of psychology have been shaped by people in times, places, and cultures that seem, on the surface, very different from our own. A brief look at some of these writers and their achievements will help us see the vital social connections that link us to all times and cultures. It also will provide us with a sense of the depth and breadth of the study of psychology, so that when we write about psychology we do so creatively and knowledgeably. The story of psychology is the story of the human race. Acquaintance with psychology's history provides a context for understanding how psychology relates to other sciences, how it plays a significant role in culture and politics, and how various theoretical conflicts within the field emerged.

Psychology probably began when the first people, experiencing dreams and visions, tried to find a way to understand themselves and explain their behavior. In ancient times "psychologists" would have been the priests, shamans, wizards, or diviners sought out by the community for their powers to give meaning to dreams and visions. Psychology is a combination of two Greek words, *psyche,* meaning soul, and *logos,* meaning word. Psychology, literally, is "words about the soul." The existence of dreams, visions, and imagination could have spawned the concept of the soul, which appears in ancient literature for at least a thousand years before the concept "mind" was clearly defined. Inscriptions known as the Book of the Dead, found on Egyptian tombs dating from 2200 B.C.E., depict the soul in association with the heart and instruct readers how to keep the soul safe as it travels after death. Milesian philosopher Thales (624–546 B.C.E), in an early attempt to understand sensation, proposed that the soul gives motion to the body. Socrates (470–399 B.C.E.) believed that reason was a process by which we may know our own souls and the ultimate truth.

Plato (427–347 B.C.E.), Socrates' most famous student, began to define intelligence when he inquired about whether memories are present at birth and speculated that memories are linked through a process of association. Plato wrote clear and powerful ethical theories and described the mind as the human capacity to reason. For Plato, reason is an ability to perceive "forms," which we would call abstract ideas. He believed that a higher realm of existence, beyond what we know in this world, can be perceived by reason. In this higher realm there exists a series of forms, perfect representations of each thing here on earth. In other words, in the higher world there are forms of men, women, trees, cats, tables, and coats, that are more perfect and more real than any particular man, woman, tree, cat, table, or coat on earth.

Plato also formulated basic scientific concepts that help us to distinguish instincts and traits with which we are born from behaviors we are taught as we grow up. His writings on the mind initiated scientific inquiries that later led to distinctions between retention and retrieval of memories. Aristotle (384–322 B.C.E.), Plato's most famous student, spoke of the human mind and behavior as being governed by natural laws, as are the stars and seas, and helped to define concepts of memory, perception, and intelligence. For both Plato and Aristotle, however, the mind was not clearly distinguished from the soul.

Early Christian and medieval thinkers developed the idea that the human soul was not as closely connected to the human body as Aristotle had thought. They perceived humans as central to God's creation, and the soul as immortal. St. Augustine (396–430 B.C.E.) recorded observations about his own development as a child, and in so doing produced a rudimentary child psychology. Through a process of self-reflection and self-observation, he differentiated distinct qualities of the soul: understanding, will, and memory. This self-reflection process provided a foundation for later research efforts that have become known as the introspective tradition in psychology. During the medieval period, psychology was mostly confined to religion. Theologians interpreted psychological phenomena in theological terms, and priests provided counseling.

Beginning with the Reformation, scientists, philosophers, and clergy studied many topics, such as love, sleep, temperament, facial expression, the circulatory system, optics, and learning, that are now considered to fall within the domain of psychology. As formalized thinking grew more sophisticated, theorists demystified bodily functions and emotions.

Historians of psychology credit German scientist Wilhelm Wundt (1832–1920) with founding the modern science of psychology as an academic *discipline* in 1879, when he began research efforts that resulted in the creation of the first psychology research laboratory, the first psychology research journals, and the first psychology textbooks. Wundt's student, Stanley Hall (1844–1924), established the American Psychological Association, and his research in lifespan development provided a foundation for the discipline of child psychology. Another of Wundt's American students, Edward Titchener (1867–1927), founded the *structuralist* school of psychology when he identified and described three basic components of the mind: feelings, images, and sensations. Structuralists study the mind by combining objective data from recorded sensory responses with subjective information obtained from emotional responses, dreams, and memories. Structuralist studies are now included within the discipline known as *cognitive psychology*, which attempts to describe how humans think and make decisions.

In contrast to the structuralists, William James (1842–1910) was more interested in the purposes of consciousness than he was in the mind's structure. His approach to the study of psychology was known as *functionalism*, which explores relationships between conscious experience and behavioral observations. Functionalism concerns itself with answering *why* something is in the consciousness, not just *what* is in the consciousness. Learning and motivation studies have developed from methods originating with functionalism.

John Watson (1878–1958) founded American *behaviorism.* Unlike functionalists, Watson focused only on physical responses that may be observed and measured. Watson denied the reliability of self-perceptions and proposed that psychologists should not be concerned with consciousness at all. B. F. Skinner (1904–1990) developed Watson's ideas further through applications of behavioral reinforcement, a technique wherein behavior is shaped toward a desired goal by rewarding subjects for exhibiting desired behaviors. Behaviorism is currently applied in programs known as behavior modification, biofeedback training, assertiveness training, and self-monitoring. In combination with cognition studies, behavioralism has spawned what is known as the *cognitive-behavioral approach.*

Another approach to understanding human behavior is called *Gestalt psychology,* named by its three founders, Max Wertheimer (1880–1943), Kurt Koffka (1886–1941), and Wolfgang Kohler (1887–1967). These German researchers believed humans see a unified whole that gives meaning to and is more than its individual parts. They rejected the behaviorists' belief that understanding can be drawn only from observable behavior and that learning takes place only mechanically. They also rejected the structuralist idea that perceptions can be explained as discrete items, separate from the whole. Gestalt psychologists believe that people achieve sudden understanding through *insight,* when pieces of information coalesce to create a meaningful whole.

The *psychoanalytic school,* founded by Sigmund Freud (1856–1939), departed from previous methods to emphasize how *unconscious* conflicts and motives can direct human behavior. Freud believed childhood experiences and sexual drives were the cause of emotional conflicts. Defense mechanisms, such as repression of painful memories, provide humans the tools to mediate unconscious desires and conscious moral strictures. Freud's student Carl Jung (1875–1961) developed a competing school of psychoanalysis based on a concept of a "collective unconsciousness" in which all people exhibit in their dreams the same patterns of archetypal images (visions that have symbolic meaning), such as snakes (representing challenge) and water (representing the subconscious mind).

What Do Psychologists Study and Why?

Psychology examines the nature of human experience and behavior, and it explains what we feel, think, and do. Almost everyone experiences anger, fear, falling in love, learning, perceiving, sensing, remembering, forgetting, being dependent, and responding to group pressure, but most people do not fully understand the origins or implications of these experiences. In their pursuit of knowledge, psychologists also study related matters such as behavior of animals and many aspects of the environments in which people live. Psychologists are convinced that Socrates was right when he said, "the unexamined life is not worth living." For psychologists the unexamined psychological life is certainly impoverished, and so we examine psychology in large and small ways through techniques developed by thousands of "scientists of the mind."

How Do We Study Psychology?

Psychologists observe and study humans by description, correlation, and experimentation. They describe human behavior through a variety of observation methods we will explain later in this book, such as experiments. Experimental studies test hypotheses (educated guesses about the nature of relationships) to determine a cause-and-effect relationship between behavioral variables, such as the extent to which anxiety causes overeating. Experimental studies form the core of the science of psychology, since the ability to determine cause and effect allows scientists to make predictions and generalizations that are necessary to develop prognoses and treatments.

Psychology is both a science and an art. In its attempts to discover general principles, locate causal factors, and explore ways in which variables are correlated or experiences described, the field of psychology is a science. In its attempts to apply general principles clinically to the specific needs of individuals, the field of psychology is an art.

An Eclectic Discipline: Psychology Today

In some ways, the goal of psychological inquiry in the twentieth century is the same as it has been from the discipline's earliest days: to understand human behavior and motivation. Now, in the twenty-first century, however, that inquiry has a complexity unimagined even forty years ago. The tools of inquiry and methodologies have become ever more sophisticated, recently through evolving computer capabilities. The research questions, however, remain essentially the same. Still fascinated with human nature, psychologists want to account for individual differences and similarities. They want to know what determines patterns of interaction, development, action, and knowing. The burgeoning number of subdisciplines reflects the explosion of information being gathered about the human condition.

Psychology in the United States is organized by the American Psychological Association, the American Psychological Society, and numerous regional and state associations that hold annual meetings at which papers are presented and discussions are held. "Program divisions" are groups within these associations organized to study a specific topic, such as individual differences, environmental issues, or geriatrics. Examining a recent list of program divisions will give some idea of the diversity of topics studied within the discipline of psychology. The 2000 annual meeting of the American Psychological Association, held in Washington, D.C. from August 4 to August 8, 2000, featured hundreds of paper presentations, round-table discussions, workshops and seminars, and poster presentations from people organized within fifty-three different program divisions:

Division 1 General Psychology
Division 2 The Society for the Teaching of Psychology
Division 3 Experimental Psychology

[No Division 4]
Division 5 Evaluation, Measurement, and Statistics
Division 6 Behavioral Neuroscience and Comparative Psychology
Division 7 Developmental Psychology
Division 8 Society for Personality and Social Psychology
Division 9 Society for the Psychological Study of Social Issues
Division 10 Psychology and the Arts
[No Division 11]
Division 12 Clinical Psychology
Division 13 Consulting Psychology
Division 14 The Society for Industrial and Organizational Psychology
Division 15 Educational Psychology
Division 16 School Psychology
Division 17 Counseling Psychology
Division 18 Psychologists in Public Service
Division 19 Military Psychology
Division 20 Adult Development and Aging
Division 21 Applied Experimental and Engineering Psychologists
Division 22 Rehabilitation Psychology
Division 23 Society for Consumer Psychology
Division 24 Theoretical and Philosophical Psychology
Division 25 Experimental Analysis of Behavior
Division 26 History of Psychology
Division 27 Society for Community Research and Action: Division
    of Community Psychology
Division 28 Psychopharmacology and Substance Abuse
Division 29 Psychotherapy
Division 30 Psychological Hypnosis
Division 31 State Psychological Association Affairs
Division 32 Humanistic Psychology
Division 33 Mental Retardation and Developmental Disabilities
Division 34 Population and Environmental Psychology
Division 35 Psychology of Women
Division 36 Psychology of Religion
Division 37 Child, Youth, and Family Services
Division 38 Health Psychology
Division 39 Psychoanalysis
Division 40 Clinical Neuropsychology
Division 41 The American Psychology-Law Society
Division 42 Psychologists in Independent Practice
Division 43 Family Psychology
Division 44 Society for the Psychological Study of Lesbian and Gay Issues
Division 45 Society for the Psychological Study of Ethnic Minority Issues
Division 46 Media Psychology
Division 47 Exercise and Sport Psychology

Division 48 Society for the Study of Peace, Conflict, and Violence:
  Peace Psychology
Division 49 Group Psychology and Group Psychotherapy
Division 50 Addictions
Division 51 The Society for the Psychological Study of Men
  and Masculinity
Division 52 International Psychology
Division 53 Clinical Child Psychology
Division 54 Society of Pediactric Psychology
Division55 American Society for the Advancement of Pharmacotherapy

The Power of Language

The discipline of psychology makes progress only because researchers express their findings in writing for other psychologists and students of psychology to read. To become an effective psychologist, you must be able to communicate not only verbally but in writing. The purpose of this book is to help you develop your ability to communicate *clearly* and *powerfully*. Influential psychologists, such as Irvin Yalom and Howard Gardner, not only developed powerful concepts but also communicated these concepts clearly in their writings.

Erich Fromm, Ph.D., gained fame as a psychologist because his writing is clear and powerful. Consider, for example, this passage from Fromm's 1964 book entitled *The Heart of Man: Its Genius for Good and Evil* (note that Fromm is writing before our present awareness of gender-neutral language):

> There are many who believe that men are sheep; there are others who believe that men are wolves. Both sides can muster good arguments for their positions. Those who propose that men are sheep have only to point to the fact that men are easily influenced to do what they are told, even if it is harmful to themselves; that they have followed their leaders into wars which brought them nothing but destruction; that they have believed any kind of nonsense if it was only presented with sufficient vigor and supported by power—from the harsh threats of priests and kings to the soft voices of the hidden and not-so-hidden persuaders. It seems that the majority of men are suggestible, half-awake children, willing to surrender their will to anyone who speaks with a voice that is threatening or sweet enough to sway them. Indeed, he who has a conviction strong enough to withstand the opposition of the crowd is the exception rather than the rule, an exception often admired centuries later, mostly laughed at by his contemporaries. (p. 7)

The use of metaphorical imagery, such as comparing people to wolves, has become a popular way to present psychological ideas. Clarissa Pinkola-Estes, Ph.D., is a Jungian analyst who has achieved national prominence through the power of her writing. Her best-selling book, *Women Who Run with the Wolves* (1992), employs narrative, that is, storytelling, as a method of communicating psychological ideas. Notice how Estes draws you into her subject by describing what she calls the "Wild Woman":

Wildlife and the Wild Woman are both endangered species. Over time, we have seen the feminine instinctive nature looted, driven back, and overbuilt. For long periods it has been mismanaged like the wildlife and the wildlands. For several thousand years, as soon and as often as we turn our backs, it is relegated to the poorest land in the psyche. The spiritual lands of Wild Woman have, throughout history, been plundered or burnt, dens bulldozed, and natural cycles forced into unnatural rhythms to please others.

It's not by accident that the pristine wilderness of our planet disappears as the understanding of our own inner wild natures fades. It is not so difficult to comprehend why old forests and old women are viewed as not very important resources. It is not such a mystery. It is not so coincidental that wolves and coyotes, bears, and wildish women have similar reputations. They all share related instinctual archetypes, and as such, both are erroneously reputed to be ungracious, wholly and innately dangerous, and ravenous. (p. 3)

After reading Estes's popular prose, you may object that serious psychology, as opposed to popular psychology, is not well served by brightly painted images of "wild women," wolves, and the magnificent images of clear mountain streams and flower-laden meadows that come to mind when we mention the natural environment. Your objection is well noted. But keep in mind two points. First, Estes has demonstrated that storytelling may be a powerful force in personal healing. Second, good writing is powerful even in more "academic" books. An academic study that illustrates both of these points is *Story Re-Visions: Narrative Therapy in the Postmodern World,* by psychologists Alan Parry and Robert Doan (1994). Parry and Doan explain that, in what has come to be known as the "post-modern" world (thanks to the writings of philosopher Jacques Derrida and others), the value of storytelling as a tool for self-understanding has been disparaged and neglected. One of the valuable discoveries of contemporary psychology, however, is the idea that as human beings we all create stories about our lives, our own versions of what has happened to us and why those things have happened:

Once upon a time, everything was understood through stories. Stories were always called upon to make things understandable. The philosopher Friedrich Nietzsche once said that "if we possess our *why* of life we can put up with almost any *how*" . . . . Stories always dealt with the "why" questions. The answers they gave did not have to be literally true; they only had to satisfy people's curiosity by providing an answer, less for the mind than for the soul. For the soul they were true, but probably no one bothered to ask whether that truth was factual or "merely" metaphorical. That question came much later.

Most of the first questions were about origins: "Why is there something and not nothing? "How did we get here?" "Who made the world, and why?" "Why did we get divided up into males and females?" "Why did trouble and sorrow enter the world?" "Why do we have to work instead of just enjoying the world's plenty?" (p.1)

Sometimes our versions of our lives contain self-defeating messages, such as, "I have always been and will always be a failure." Building upon theories developed by Australian psychologist Michael White, Parry and Doan discuss ways in which therapists can help their clients to rewrite their own life stories by re-visioning themselves as creative and capable human beings. As you read the passage from *Story Re-Visions* below, notice not only the potential power of the ideas that Parry and Doan discuss, but also the style of writing. Making complex ideas understandable is the most important characteristic of good academic writing. Although Parry and Doan discuss complex and sophisticated concepts, they do so in a manner that is readily understood even by people who have minimal knowledge of psychology:

> Before people can be free to choose which of their multitude of stories they wish to be identified with, it is therapeutically imperative that they be freed from the tyranny of those stories lurking behind the story of frustration that families and individuals bring to therapy. . . .
>
> When people use the popular expression of "pushing each other's buttons," we suggest that those "buttons" will invariably be connected to the painful memory of a story associated with each person's sense of having had to struggle for psychological survival. Each old story is what gives the current "stuck story" its driving urgency. Nor is it enough simply to identify an old story as the "reason" a person is currently behaving so defensively. . . .
>
> The old story, rather, is best brought forth in graphic detail and shown to each person as one in which a struggle for psychological survival was at stake. The therapeutic goal is not to supply reasons or offer explanations, but to awaken compassion in each person toward the other person and toward the self. (p.28)

1 Writing as Communication

1.1 Writing to Learn

Writing is a way of ordering your experience. Think about it. No matter what you are writing—it may be a paper for your Introduction to Psychology class, a short story, a limerick, a grocery list—you are putting pieces of your world together in new ways and making yourself freshly conscious of these pieces. This is one of the reasons why writing is so hard. From the infinite welter of data that your mind continually processes and locks in your memory, you are selecting only certain items significant to the task at hand, relating them to other items, and phrasing them in a new coherence. You are mapping a part of your universe that has hitherto been unknown territory. You are gaining a little more control over the processes by which you interact with the world around you.

This is why the act of writing, no matter what its result, is never insignificant. It is always *communication*, if not with another human being, then with yourself. It is a way of making a fresh connection with your world.

Writing, therefore, is also one of the best ways to learn. This statement at first may sound odd. If you are an unpracticed writer, you may share a common notion that the only purpose of writing is to express what you already know or think. According to this view, any learning that you as a writer might have experienced has already occurred by the time your pen meets the paper; your task is to inform and even surprise the reader. But if you are a practiced writer, you know that at any moment as you write you are capable of surprising *yourself*. And it is surprise that you look for: the shock of seeing what happens in your own mind when you drop an old, established opinion into a batch of new facts or bump into a cherished belief from a different angle. Writing synthesizes new understanding for the writer. E. M. Forester's famous question, "How do I know what I think until I see what I say?" is one that all of us could ask. We make meaning as we write, jolting ourselves by little discoveries into a larger and more interesting universe.

The Irony of Writing

Good writing, especially good writing about psychology, helps the reader become aware of the ironies and paradoxes of human existence. One such paradox is that good writing, like good art, expresses both what is unique about the writer and what the writer shares with every human being. Many interesting psychological statements share this double attribute of mirroring the singular and the ordinary simultaneously. For example, consider psychologist Rollo May's explanation of how artists creatively represent objects in ways that are both unique and universal. Consider further how May's own well-written description of this process accomplishes the paradoxical unity of uniqueness and universality:

> [French painter Paul] Cezanne sees a tree. He sees it in a way no one else has ever seen it. He experiences, as he no doubt would have said, "being grasped by the tree." The arching grandeur of the tree, the mothering spread, the delicate balance as the tree grips the earth—all these and many more characteristics of the tree are absorbed into his perception and are felt throughout his nervous structure. These are part of the vision he experiences. This vision involves an omission of some aspects of the scene and a greater emphasis on other aspects and the ensuing rearrangement of the whole; but it is more than the sum of all these. Primarily it is a vision that is now not the tree, but Tree; the concrete tree Cezanne looked at is formed into the essence of tree. However original and unrepeatable his vision is, it is still a vision of all trees triggered by his encounter with this particular one.
>
> The painting that issues out of this encounter between a human being, Cezanne, and an objective reality, the tree, is literally new, unique and original. Something is born, comes into being, something that did not exist before—which is as good a definition of creativity as we can get. Thereafter everyone who looks at the painting with intensity of awareness and lets it speak to him or her will see the tree with the unique powerful movement, the intimacy between the tree and the landscape, and the architectural beauty which literally did not exist in our relation with trees until Cezanne experienced and painted them. I can say without exaggeration that I never really *saw* a tree until I had seen and absorbed Cezanne's paintings of them. (pp. 77–78)

Good writing does for our understanding of psychology what Cezanne's representation of a tree does for our perception of trees. As thousands of readers can attest, works written by incisive, keenly observant psychologists help us all to see the meanings behind the varieties of human experience.

The help that writing gives us with learning and with controlling what we learn is one of the major reasons why your psychology instructors will require a great deal of writing from you. Learning the complex and diverse world of the psychologist takes more than a passive assimilation of facts. You have to understand emotion, memory, stimulus response, and many more mental processes, and you must come to grips with conflicting theories and interpretations of them. When you write a paper in a class on experimental psychology or the psychology of adolescence, you are entering into the world of psychologists in the same way they do—by testing theory against fact, fact against belief.

Writing is the means of entering psychological life. Virtually everything that contributes to our knowledge of psychology happens eventually on paper. Documents are wrestled into shape before their contents can spread the news of discoveries. Often, in psychology as elsewhere, gaining recognition for our ourselves and our ideas depends less upon what we say than upon how we say it. Accurate and persuasive writing is absolutely vital to the psychologist.

Exercise *Learning by Writing*

A way of testing the notion that writing is a powerful learning tool is by rewriting your notes from a recent class lecture. The type of class does not matter; it can be psychology, but the same principles apply to history, chemistry, advertising, whatever. If possible, choose a difficult class, one in which you are feeling somewhat unsure of the material and for which you have taken copious notes.

As you rewrite, provide the transitional elements (connecting phrases such as *in order to, because of, and, but, however*) that you were unable to supply in class because of the press of time. Furnish your own examples or illustrations of the ideas expressed in the lecture.

This experiment will force you to supply necessary coherence to your own thought processes. See if your increased understanding of the lecture material does not more than compensate for the time it takes you to rewrite the notes.

Challenge Yourself

There is no way around it: Writing is a struggle. Did you think you were the only one to feel this way? Take heart! Writing is hard for everybody, great writers included. Bringing order to the world is never easy. Isaac Bashevis Singer, winner of the 1978 Nobel Prize in literature, once wrote, "I believe in miracles in every area of life *except* writing. Experience has shown me that there are no miracles in writing. The only thing that produces good writing is hard work" (quoted in Lunsford and Connors, 1992, p. 2).

Effective prose is so clear and easily understood that it appears effortless, but only hard work can make it so. Consider Erich Fromm's (1967) introduction to his book *Psychoanalysis and Religion:*

> Never before has man come so close to the fulfillment of his most cher-
> ished hopes as today. Our scientific discoveries and technical achievements en-
> able us to visualize the day when the table will be set for all who want to eat, a
> day when the human race will form a unified community and no longer live as
> separate entities. Thousands of years were needed for this unfolding of man's
> intellectual capacities, of his growing ability to organize society and to concen-
> trate his energies purposefully. Man has created a new world with its own laws
> and destiny. Looking at his creation, he can say, truly, it is good.
>
> But looking at himself what can he say? Has he come closer to the real-
> ization of another dream of mankind, that of the perfection of man; of man
> loving his neighbor, doing justice, speaking truth, and realizing that which
> he potentially is, an image of God?
>
> Raising the question is embarrassing since the answer is so painfully
> clear. While we have created wonderful things we have failed to make of our-
> selves beings for whom this tremendous effort would seem worthwhile. Ours
> is a life not of brotherliness, happiness, contentment but of spiritual chaos
> and bewilderment dangerously close to a state of madness—not the hysteri-
> cal kind of madness which existed in the Middle Ages but a madness akin to
> schizophrenia in which the contact with inner reality is lost and thought is
> split from affect. (pp. 1–2)

One reason that writing is difficult is that it is not actually a single activity
at all but a process consisting of several activities that can overlap, with two or
more sometimes operating *simultaneously* as you labor to organize and phrase
your thoughts. (We will discuss these activities later in this chapter.) The writing
process tends to be sloppy for everyone, an often frustrating search for meaning
and for the best way to articulate that meaning.

Frustrating though that search may sometimes be, it need not be futile. Remember this: The writing process uses skills that we all have. The ability to write,
in other words, is not some magical competence bestowed on the rare, fortu-
nate individual. While few of us may achieve the proficiency of Isaac Bashevis
Singer or Erich Fromm, we are all capable of phrasing thoughts clearly and in a
well-organized fashion. But learning how to do so takes *practice*.

The one sure way to improve your writing is to write.

One of the toughest but most important jobs in writing is to maintain enthusiasm for your writing project. Such commitment may sometimes be hard to
achieve, given the difficulties that are inherent in the writing process and that
can be made worse when the project is unappealing at first glance. How, for example, can you be enthusiastic about having to write a paper analyzing the behavior of a molecule when you can see no relationship between the molecule's
behavior and your own?

One of the worst mistakes that unpracticed student writers make is to fail
to assume responsibility for keeping themselves interested in their writing. No
matter how hard it may seem at first to drum up interest in your topic, *you have
to do it*—that is, if you want to write a paper you can be proud of, one that contributes useful material and a fresh point of view to the topic. One thing is guaranteed: If you are bored with your writing, your reader will be, too. So what can
you do to keep your interest and energy level high?

Challenge yourself. Think of the paper not as an assignment but as a piece of writing that has a point to make. To get this point across persuasively is the real reason why you are writing, *not* the simple fact that a teacher has assigned you a project. If someone were to ask you why you are writing your paper and your immediate, unthinking response is, "Because I've been given a writing assignment," or "Because I want a good grade," or some other non-answer along these lines, your paper may be in trouble.

If, on the other hand, your first impulse is to explain the challenge of your main point—"I'm writing to explain how depression affects people in a work environment"—then you are thinking usefully about your topic.

Maintain Self-Confidence

Having confidence in your ability to write well about your topic is essential for good writing. This does not mean that you will always know what the result of a particular writing activity will be. In fact, you have to cultivate your ability to tolerate a high degree of uncertainty while weighing evidence, testing hypotheses, and experimenting with organizational strategies and wording. Be ready for temporary confusion and for seeming dead ends, and remember that every writer faces these obstacles. It is from your struggle to combine fact with fact, to buttress conjecture with evidence, that order arises.

Do not be intimidated by the amount and quality of work that others have already done in your field of inquiry. The array of opinion and evidence that confronts you in the literature can be confusing. But remember that no important topic is ever exhausted. *There are always gaps*—questions that have not been satisfactorily explored in either the published research or the prevailing popular opinion. It is in these gaps that you establish your own authority, your own sense of control.

Remember that the various stages of the writing process reinforce each other. Establishing a solid motivation strengthens your sense of confidence about the project, which in turn influences how successfully you organize and write. If you start out well, use good work habits, and give yourself ample time for the various activities to coalesce, you should produce a paper that will reflect your best work, one that your audience will find both readable and useful.

1.2 The Writing Process

The Nature of the Process

As you engage in the writing process, you are doing many things at once. While planning, you are no doubt defining the audience for your paper at the same time that you are thinking about its purpose. As you draft the paper, you may organize your next sentence while revising the one you have just written. Different parts of the writing process overlap, and much of the difficulty of writing occurs because so many things happen at once. Through practice—in other words, through *writing*—it is possible to learn how to control those parts of the process that can in fact be controlled and to encourage those mysterious, less controllable activities.

No two people go about writing in exactly the same way. It is important to recognize the routines—modes of thought as well as individual exercises—that help you negotiate the process successfully. It is also important to give yourself as much time as possible to complete the process. Procrastination is one of the writer's greatest enemies. It saps confidence, undermines energy, destroys concentration. Writing regularly and following a well-planned schedule often make the difference between a successful paper and an embarrassment.

Although the various parts of the writing process are interwoven, there is naturally a general order to the work of writing. You have to start somewhere! What follows is a description of the various stages of the writing process—*planning, drafting, revising, editing, proofreading*—along with suggestions on how to approach each most successfully.

Planning

Planning includes all activities that lead to the writing of the first draft of a paper. The particular activities in this stage differ from person to person. Some writers, for instance, prefer to compile a formal outline before writing the draft. Others perform brief writing exercises to jump start their imaginations. Some draw diagrams; some doodle. Later we will look at a few starting strategies, and you can determine which of them may help you.

Now, however, let us discuss certain early choices that all writers must make during the planning stage. These choices concern *topic, purpose,* and *audience,* elements that make up the *writing context,* or the terms under which we all write. Every time you write, even if you are only writing a diary entry or a note to a friend, these elements are present. You may not give conscious consideration to all of them in each piece of writing that you do, but it is extremely important to think carefully about them when writing a psychology paper. Some or all of these defining elements may be dictated by your assignment, yet you will always have a degree of control over them.

Selecting a Topic

No matter how restrictive an assignment may seem, there is no reason to feel trapped by it. Within any assigned subject you can find a range of topics to explore. What you are looking for is a topic that engages your *own* interest. Let your curiosity be your guide. If, for example, you have been assigned the subject "biological processes of memory," then guide yourself to find some issue concerning the biological processes of memory that interests you. (What can cause memory to lapse? What environmental influences enhance memory?) You may well find that your interest increases if you simply begin asking questions; any good topic comes with a set or two. One strong recommendation: Ask your questions *on paper*. Like most mental activities, the process of exploring your way through a topic is transformed when you write down your thoughts as they come instead of letting them fly through your mind unrecorded. Remember the words of Louis Agassiz: "A pen is often the best of eyes" (p. 106).

While it is vital to be interested in your topic, you do not have to know much about it at the outset of your investigation. In fact, having too heartfelt a commitment to a topic can be an impediment to writing about it; emotions can get in the way of objectivity. Better often to choose a topic that has piqued your interest yet remained something of a mystery to you, a topic discussed in one of your classes, perhaps, or mentioned on television or in a conversation with friends.

Narrowing a Topic

The task of narrowing your topic offers you a tremendous opportunity to establish a measure of control over the writing project. It is up to you to hone your topic to just the right shape and size to suit both your own interests and the requirements of the assignment. Do a good job of it, and you will go a long way toward guaranteeing yourself sufficient motivation and confidence for the tasks ahead. If you do not do this well, somewhere along the way you may find yourself directionless and out of energy.

Generally, the first topics that come to your mind will be too large for you to handle in your research paper. For example, the subject of bulimia has generated many news reports. Despite all the attention, there is still plenty of room for you to investigate the topic on a level that has real meaning to you and that does not merely recapitulate the published research. What about an analysis of the strengths and weaknesses of a particular course of treatment?

The problem with most topics is not that they are too narrow or have been too completely explored, but rather that they are so rich that it is often difficult to choose the most useful way to address them. Take some time to narrow your topic. Think through the possibilities that occur to you and, as always, jot down your thoughts.

Students in an undergraduate course on counseling therapies were told to write an essay of 2,500 words on one of the following topics. Next to each general topic is an example of how students narrowed it to make it manageable.

GENERAL TOPIC	NARROWED TOPIC
Gestalt Therapy	The Gestalt Need-Fulfillment Cycle
Behavior Therapy	Multimodal behavior therapy in marital counseling
Psychoanalysis	Psychoanalytical treatment of agoraphobia
Adlerian Therapy	Diagnostic interviews: An Adlerian approach
Reality Therapy	The importance of control theory in reality therapy

| Exercise | *Narrowing Topics* |

Without doing research, see how you can narrow the following general topics:

EXAMPLE

GENERAL TOPIC   NARROWED TOPICS

Problems for Adolescents   Peer Pressure

                            Physical Changes

                            Relationships with Parents

GENERAL TOPICS

The Nervous System	Maturation
Audition	Temperament
Facial Expression	Bereavement
Consciousness	Gender
Operant Conditioning	Defense Mechanisms
Memory	Anxiety
Learning	Schizophrenia
Language	Psychosurgery
Stress	

Finding a Thesis

As you plan your writing, be on the lookout for an idea that can serve as your *thesis*. A thesis is not a fact, which can be immediately verified by data, but an assertion worth discussing, an argument with more than one possible conclusion. Your thesis sentence will reveal to your reader not only the argument you have chosen, but also your orientation toward it and the conclusion that your paper will attempt to prove.

In looking for a thesis, you are doing many jobs at once:

1. You are limiting the amount and kind of material that you must cover, thus making it manageable.
2. You are increasing your own interest in the narrowing field of study.
3. You are working to establish your paper's purpose, the *reason* why you are writing about your topic. (If the only reason you can see for writing is to earn a good grade, then you probably won't!)
4. You are establishing your notion of who your readers are and what sort of approach to the subject might best catch their interest.

In short, you are gaining control over your writing context. For this reason, it is a good idea to come up with a thesis early, a *working thesis,* which will very probably change as your thinking deepens but which will allow you establish a measure of order in the planning stage.

The Thesis Sentence.   The introduction of your paper will contain a sentence that expresses the task that you intend to accomplish. This *thesis sentence* communicates your main idea, the one you are going to prove, defend, or illustrate. It sets up an expectation in the reader's mind that it is your job to satisfy. But in the planning stage, a thesis sentence is more than just the statement that informs your reader of your goal. It is a valuable tool to help you narrow your focus and confirm in your own mind your paper's purpose.

Developing a Thesis

Students in a social psychology class were assigned a twenty-page paper on a problem currently being faced by divorced women who have school-aged children. The choice of the specific problem was left to the students. One, Jean MacKay, decided to investigate problems related to forming romantic relationships. She began by developing an initial hypothesis, a tentative thesis that, if she could find enough evidence to support it, would eventually become the thesis of her paper:

> Having children sometimes makes it more difficult for divorced women to form romantic relationships.

The problem with this thesis, as Jean found out, was that it was not an idea that could be argued, but rather a fact that could be easily corroborated by the sources Jean began to consult. As she read research studies and talked with some of her friends who were divorced and had children, she began to get interested in people's expectations when they meet prospective romantic partners. Jean's second working thesis was as follows:

> When meeting prospective romantic partners, divorced women with children often expect their children to be a liability to the relationship.

Her second thesis narrowed the topic somewhat and gave Jean an opportunity to use material from her research, but there was still no real comment attached to it. It still stated a bare fact, easily proved. At this point, Jean became interested in the even narrower topic of how women might manage to make their children an asset to the romantic relationship. She found that the major issue was a woman's expectations regarding acceptance of her children by the partner. As Jean explored relevant studies, she began to develop a third working thesis:

Women who expect prospective romantic partners to take an immediate positive interest in their children have more difficulty in forming romantic relationships than women who do not share this expectation.

Note how this thesis narrows the focus of Jean's paper even further than the other two while also presenting an arguable hypothesis. It tells Jean what she has to do in her paper, just as it tells her readers what to expect.

At some time during your preliminary thinking on a topic, you should consult the library to see how much published work on your issue exists. This search has at least two benefits:

1. It acquaints you with a body of writing that will become very important in the research phase of your paper.
2. It gives you a sense of how your topic is generally addressed by the community of scholars you are joining. Is the topic as important as you think it is? Has there been so much research on the subject as to make your inquiry, in its present formulation, irrelevant?

As you go about determining your topic, remember that one goal of writing is to enhance your own understanding of the psychological process, to build an accurate model of the way psychology works. Let this goal help you aim your research into those areas that you know are important to your knowledge of the discipline.

Learn what you want to say. By the time you write your final draft, you must have a very sound notion of the point you wish to argue. If, as you write that final draft, someone were to ask you to state your thesis, you should be able to give a satisfactory answer with a minimum of delay and no prompting. If, on the other hand, you have to hedge your answer because you cannot easily express your thesis, you may not yet be ready to write a final draft. You may have to write a draft or two or engage in various prewriting activities in order to arrive at a secure understanding of your task.

| *Exercise* | *Knowing What You Want to Say* |

Two writers have been asked to state the thesis of their papers. Which one better understands the writing task?

WRITER 1   My paper is about menopause.

WRITER 2   My paper demonstrates that menopause lessens women's sexual interest.

Watch out for bias! There is no such thing as pure objectivity. You are not a machine. No matter how hard you may try to produce an objective paper, the fact is that every choice you make as you write is influenced to some extent by your personal beliefs and opinions. In other words, what you present to your readers as the truth is influenced, sometimes without your knowing, by a multitude of factors, including your environment, upbringing, and education; your attitude toward your audience; your psychological affiliation; your race and gender; your career goals; and your ambitions for the paper you are writing. The influence of such factors can be very subtle, and it is something you must work to identify in your own writing as well as in the writing of others in order not to mislead or be misled. Remember that one of the reasons for writing is *self-discovery.* The writing you will do in psychology classes—as well as the writing you will do for the rest of your life—will give you a chance to discover and confront honestly your own views on your subjects. Responsible writers keep an eye on their own biases and are honest about them with their readers.

Defining Your Audience

In any class that requires you to write, it may sometimes be difficult to remember that the point of your writing is not simply to jump through the technical hoops imposed by the assignment. The point is to *communicate*—to transmit your knowledge and your conclusions to the readers in a way that suits you. Your task is to pass on to your readers the spark of your own enthusiasm for your topic. Readers who were indifferent to your topic before reading your paper should look at it in a new way after finishing the paper. This is the great challenge of writing: to enter into a reader's mind and leave behind both new knowledge *and* new questions.

It is tempting to think that most writing problems would be solved if the writer could view the writing as if it had been produced by another person. The discrepancy between the understanding of the writer and that of the audience is the single greatest impediment to accurate communication. To overcome this barrier you must consider your audience's needs. By the time you begin drafting, most if not all of your ideas will have begun to attain coherent shape in your mind, so that virtually any words with which you try to express those ideas will reflect your thought accurately—*to you.* Your readers, however, do not already hold the conclusions that you have so painstakingly achieved. If you omit from your writing the material that is necessary to complete your readers' understanding of your argument, they may well not be able to supply that information themselves.

The potential for misunderstanding is present for any audience, whether it is made up of general readers, experts in the field, or your professor, who is reading in part to see how well you have mastered the constraints that govern the relationship between writer and reader. Make your presentation as complete as possible, bearing in mind your audience's knowledge—or lack of knowledge—about your topic.

Using Invention Strategies

We have discussed various methods of selecting and narrowing the topic of a paper. As your focus on a specific topic sharpens, you will naturally begin to think about the kinds of information that will go into the paper. In the case of papers not requiring formal research, that material will come largely from your own recollections. Indeed, one of the reasons instructors assign such papers is to convince you of the incredible richness of your memory, the vastness and variety of the "database" you have accumulated and that, moment by moment, you continue to build.

So vast is your horde of information that it can sometimes be difficult to select from within it the material that would best suit your paper. In other words, finding out what you already know about a topic is not always easy. *Invention,* a term borrowed from classical rhetoric, refers to the task of discovering, or recovering from memory, such information. As we write, we go through some sort of invention procedure that helps us explore our topic. Some writers seem to have little problem coming up with material; others need more help. Over the centuries writers have devised different exercises that can help locate useful material housed in memory. We shall look at a few of these briefly.

Freewriting

Freewriting is an activity that forces you to get something down on paper. There is no waiting around for inspiration. Instead, you set a time limit—perhaps three minutes or five minutes—and write for that length of time without stopping, not even to lift the pen from the paper or your hands from the keyboard. Focus on the topic, and do not let the difficulty of finding relevant material stop you from writing. If necessary, you may begin by writing, over and over, some seemingly useless phrase, such as "I cannot think of anything to write," or perhaps the name of your topic. Eventually, something else will occur to you. (It is surprising how long a three-minute period of freewriting can seem to last!) At the end of the freewriting, look over what you have produced for anything you might be able to use. Much of the writing will be unusable, but there may be an insight or two that you did not know you possessed.

In addition to its ability to help you recover from your memory usable material for your paper, freewriting has certain other benefits. First, it takes little time, which means you may repeat the exercise as often as you like. Second, it breaks down some of the resistance that stands between you and the act of writing. There is no initial struggle to find something to say. You just *write.*

Freewriting

For her second-year Introduction to Psychology class, Shirley Quint had to write a paper on some aspect of child development. Shirley, who felt her understanding of child development was slight, began the job of finding a topic that interested her with two minutes of freewriting. Thinking about local children, Shirley wrote steadily for this period without lifting her pen from the paper. Here is the result of her freewriting:

> *Development Development. What does that mean? Like growing up? Getting smarter? Facing bigger kids? I was a fat kid and the others made fun of me. Called me "Porky." I got used to it, I guess. They always let me play with them, though, even if I was not much good at sports, they let me play. Maybe find out what happens to fat kids, how they do in school as compared to normal kids. Trace what happens to fat kids. I wonder if there are any case studies. I wonder if there are any statistics. I wonder if their problems are like those of other kids who are different—black kids in white neighborhoods—kids with physical challenges. Point would be, what? Point point point. To find out how different it is to be a fat kid, and if their problems are the same as other kids who seem to be different from the rest in some way. Do they do less well in school? Do they have more mental health problems? Lots of research to do. Where to start? Where*

Brainstorming

Brainstorming is simply making a list of ideas about a topic. It can be done quickly and at first without any need to order items into a coherent pattern. The point is to write down everything that occurs to you as quickly and briefly as possible, using individual words or short phrases. Once you have a good-sized list of items, you can then group them according to relationships that you see among them. Brainstorming thus allows you to uncover both ideas stored in your memory and useful associations among those ideas.

Brainstorming

A professor in a "human intelligence" class asked his students to write a ten-page paper on any aspect of intelligence that personally intrigued the student. One student, Jose Xalaca, started thinking about the assignment by brainstorming. First, he simply wrote down anything about intelligence that occurred to him:

smart	*perception*	*insight*
understanding	*creativity variety*	*types of*
meaning	*analytical*	*intelligence*
motor skills sports	*abstractions*	*art*
architecture	*mathematics*	*music*

Thinking through his list, Jose recalled that he had heard someone say that people who are gifted in music are also often good at mathematics. Because he had interests in both these subjects, he decided to study the relationship between aptitude for mathematics and aptitude for music.

Asking Questions

It is always possible to ask most or all of the following questions about any topic: *Who? What? When? Where? Why? How?* They force you to approach the topic as a journalist does, setting it within different perspectives that can then be compared.

Asking Questions

A professor asked her students in her class on learning to write a paper describing how they experience classical conditioning in their own lives. One student developed the following questions as he began to think about a thesis:

How can I discover my own classical conditioning?

In what forms might it appear?

Who can I get to help me?

What are the varieties of conditioning?

Who has done some good studies?

To what stimuli do I quickly respond?

Do I have positive or negative associations with sounds, smells, words?

Can you think of other questions that would make for useful inquiry?

Maintaining Flexibility

As you engage in invention strategies, you are also performing other writing tasks. You are still narrowing your topic, for example, as well as making decisions that will affect your choice of tone or audience. You are moving forward on all fronts, with each decision you make affecting the others. This means you must be flexible enough to allow for slight adjustments in your understanding of the paper's development and of your goal. Never be so determined to prove a particular theory that you fail to notice when your own understanding of it changes. *Stay objective.*

Organizing Your Writing

A paper that contains all the necessary facts but presents them in an ineffective order will confuse rather than inform or persuade. While there are various methods of grouping ideas, none is potentially more effective than *outlining*. Unfortunately, no organizing process is more often misunderstood.

Outlining for Yourself

Outlining can do two jobs. First, it can force you, the writer, to gain a better understanding of your ideas by arranging them according to their interrelationships. There is one primary rule of outlining: Ideas of equal weight are placed on the same level within the outline. This rule requires you to determine the relative importance of your ideas. You have to decide which ideas are of the same type or order and into which subtopic each idea best fits.

If, in the planning stage, you carefully arrange your ideas in a coherent outline, your grasp of your topic will be greatly enhanced. You will have linked your ideas logically together and given a basic structure to the body of the paper. This sort of subordinating and coordinating activity is difficult, however, and as a result inexperienced writers sometimes begin to write their first draft without an effective outline, hoping for the best. This hope is usually unfulfilled, especially in complex papers involving research.

Exercise   *Organizing Thoughts*

Preston, a student in a class in motivation and emotion, researched the satisfaction that people gain from accomplishing a goal, and he developed a number of statements about his findings. Number them in logical order:

____ The amount of satisfaction is positively correlated to the importance of the goal.

____ There are several sources of satisfaction for achieving goals.

____ The amount of satisfaction is positively correlated to the difficulty of reaching the goal.

____ The social desirability of reaching a goal is less important than recognition for achieving the goal.

____ The amount of satisfaction is positively correlated to recognition for achieving the goal.

____ The amount of satisfaction is positively correlated to the social desirability of reaching the goal.

Outlining for Your Reader

The second job an outline can perform is to serve as a reader's blueprint to the paper, summarizing its points and their interrelationships. A busy reader can quickly get a sense of your paper's goal and the argument you have used to promote it by consulting your outline. The clarity and coherence of the outline helps determine how much attention your audience will give to your ideas.

As psychology students, you will be given a great deal of help with the arrangement of your material into an outline to accompany your paper. A look at the models presented in this manual will show you how strictly these formal outlines are structured. But while you must pay close attention to these requirements, do not forget how powerful a tool an outline can be in the early planning stages of your paper.

The Formal Outline Pattern

Following this pattern of subordination and coordination during the planning stage of your paper helps to guarantee that your ideas are placed logically:

Thesis sentence (precedes the formal outline)

I. First main idea
  A. First subordinate idea
    1. Reason, example, or illustration
      a. Supporting detail
      b. Supporting detail
      c. Supporting detail
    2. Reason, example, or illustration
      a. Supporting detail
      b. Supporting detail
      c. Supporting detail
  B. Second subordinate idea
II. Second main idea

Notice that each level of the paper must have more than one entry; for every *A* there must be at least a *B* (and, if required, a *C, D,* etc.), and for every *1* there must be a *2*. This arrangement forces you to compare ideas, looking carefully at each one to determine its place among the others. The insistence on assigning relative values to your ideas is what makes an outline an effective organizing tool.

The Patterns of Psychology Papers

The structure of any particular type of psychology paper is governed by a formal pattern. When rigid external controls are placed on their writing, some writers feel that their creativity is impeded by a kind of "paint-by-numbers" approach to structure. It is vital to the success of your paper that you never allow yourself to be overwhelmed by the pattern rules for any type of paper. Remember that such controls exist not to limit your creativity but to make the paper immediately and easily useful to its intended audience. It is as necessary to write clearly and confidently in a psychology paper as in a term paper for English literature, a résumé, a short story, or a job application letter.

Drafting

The Rough Draft

The planning stage of the writing process is followed by the writing of the first draft. Using your thesis and outline as direction markers, you must now weave your amalgam of ideas, data, and persuasion strategies into logically ordered sentences and paragraphs. Although adequate prewriting may facilitate the drafting, it still will not be easy. Writers establish their own individual methods of encouraging themselves to forge ahead with the draft, but here are some tips.

1. *Remember that this is a rough draft,* not the final paper. At this stage, it is not necessary that every word be the best possible choice. Do not put that sort of pressure on yourself; you must not allow anything to slow you down now. Writing is not like sculpting in stone, where every chip is permanent. You can always go back to your draft and add, delete, reword, and rearrange. *No matter how much effort you have put into planning, you cannot be sure how much of this first draft you will eventually keep.* It may take several drafts to get one that you find satisfactory.

2. *Give yourself sufficient time to write.* Don't delay the first draft by telling yourself there is still more research to do. You cannot uncover all the material there is to know on a particular subject, so don't fool yourself into trying. Remember that writing is a process of discovery. You may have to begin writing before you can see exactly what sort of research you need to do. Keep in mind that there are other tasks waiting for you after the first draft is finished, so allow for them as you determine your writing schedule.

It is also very important to give yourself time to write because the more time that passes after you have written a draft, the better your ability to view it with greater objectivity. It is very difficult to evaluate your writing accurately soon after you complete it. You need to cool down, to recover from the effort of putting all those words together. The "colder" you get on your writing, the better able you are to read it as if it were written by someone else and thus acknowledge the changes you will need to make to strengthen the paper.

3. *Stay sharp.* Keep in mind the plan you created as you narrowed your topic, composed a thesis sentence, and outlined the material. But if you begin to feel a strong need to change the plan a bit, do not be afraid to do so. Be ready for surprises dealt you by your own growing understanding of your topic. Your goal is to record your best thinking on the subject as accurately as possible.

Language Choices

To be convincing, your writing has to be *authoritative.* That is, you have to sound as if you have complete confidence in your ability to convey your ideas in words. Sentences that sound stilted, or that suffer from weak phrasing or the use of clichés, are not going to win supporters for the positions that you express in your paper. So a major question becomes: How can I sound confident?

Here are some points to consider as you work to convey to your reader that necessary sense of authority.

Level of Formality.   Tone is one of the primary methods by which you signal to readers who you are and what your attitude is toward them and toward your topic. Your major decision is which level of language formality is most appropriate to your audience. The informal tone you would use in a letter to a friend might well be out of place in a paper on multiple identities written for a class in psychological disorders. Remember that tone is only part of the overall decision that you make about how to present your information. Formality is, to some extent, a function of individual word choices and phrasing. For example, is it appropriate to use contractions such as *isn't* or *they'll?* Would the strategic use of a sentence fragment for effect be out of place? The use of informal language, the personal *I*, and the second person *you* is traditionally forbidden—for better or worse—in certain kinds of writing. Often part of the challenge of writing a formal paper is simply how to give your prose impact while staying within the conventions.

Jargon.   One way to lose readers quickly is to overwhelm them with jargon—phrases that have a special, usually technical meaning within your discipline but that are unfamiliar to the average reader. The very occasional use of jargon may add an effective touch of atmosphere, but anything more than that will severely dampen a reader's enthusiasm for the paper. Often the writer uses jargon in an effort to impress the reader by sounding lofty or knowledgeable. Unfortunately, all jargon usually does is cause confusion. In fact, the use of jargon indicates a writer's lack of connection to the audience.

Psychology writing is a haven for jargon. Perhaps writers of psychology papers believe their readers are all completely attuned to their terminology. Or some may hope to obscure damaging information or potentially unpopular ideas in confusing language. In other cases the problem could simply be unclear thinking by the writer. Whatever the reason, the fact is that psychology papers too often sound like prose made by machines to be read by machines.

Students may feel that, in order to be accepted as psychologists, their papers should conform to the practices of their published peers. *This is a mistake.* Remember that it is never better to write a cluttered or confusing sentence than a clear one and that burying your ideas in jargon defeats the effort that you went through to form them.

Clichés.   In the heat of composition, as you are looking for words to help you form your ideas, it is sometimes easy to plug in a cliché—a phrase that has attained universal recognition by overuse.

NOTE. Clichés differ from jargon in that clichés are part of the general public's everyday language, while jargon is specific to the language of experts in a particular field. Our vocabularies are brimming with clichés:

> It's *raining cats and dogs.*
>
> That issue is *dead as a doornail.*
>
> It's time for the pedophile to *face the music.*
>
> In her last binge Amy *made a beeline* for the refrigerator.

The problem with clichés is that they are virtually meaningless. Once colorful means of expression, they have lost their color through overuse, and they tend to bleed energy and color from the surrounding words. When revising, replace clichés with fresh wording that more accurately conveys your point.

Descriptive Language. Language that appeals to the readers' senses will always engage their interest more fully than language that is abstract. This is especially important for writing in disciplines that tend to deal in abstracts, such as psychology. The typical psychology paper, with its discussions of principles and statistics, is usually in danger of floating off into abstraction, with each paragraph drifting farther away from the felt life of the readers. Whenever appropriate, appeal to your readers' sense of sight, hearing, taste, touch, or smell.

Exercise   *Using Descriptive Language*

Which of these two sentences is more effective?

1. Martha's house had deteriorated badly since the social worker's last visit.
2. Martha's house had deteriorated badly since the social worker's last visit; stench rose from the plumbing, grime coated the walls and floors, and rats scurried through the hallways.

Sexist Language. Language can be a very powerful tool for either reinforcing or destroying cultural stereotypes. By treating the sexes in subtly different ways in your language, you may unknowingly be committing an act of discrimination. A common example is the use of the pronoun *he* to refer to a person whose gender has not been identified.

Some writers, faced with this dilemma, alternate the use of male and female personal pronouns; others use the plural to avoid the need to use a pronoun of either gender:

SEXIST: A therapist should always treat his client with respect.

NONSEXIST: A therapist should always treat his or her client with respect.

NONSEXIST: Therapists should always treat their clients with respect.

SEXIST: Man is a violent creature.

NONSEXIST: People are violent creatures.

Remember that language is more than the mere vehicle of your thought. Your words shape perceptions for your readers. How well you say something will profoundly affect your readers' response to what you say. Sexist language denies to a large number of your readers the basic right to fair and equal treatment. Make sure your writing is not guilty of this form of discrimination.

Revising

Revising is one of the most important steps in assuring the success of your essay. While unpracticed writers often think of revision as little more than making sure all the *i*'s are dotted and *t*'s are crossed, it is much more than that. Revising is *reseeing* the essay, looking at it from other perspectives, trying always to align your view with the one that will be held by your audience. Research indicates that we are actually revising all the time, in every phase of the writing process as we reread phrases, rethink the placement of an item in an outline, or test a new topic sentence for a paragraph. Subjecting your entire hard-fought draft to cold, objective scrutiny is one of the toughest activities to master, but it is absolutely necessary. You have to make sure that you have said everything that needs to be said clearly and logically. One confusing passage, and the reader's attention is deflected from where you want it to be. Suddenly the reader has to become a detective, trying to figure out why you wrote what you did and what you meant by it. You do not want to throw such obstacles in the path of understanding.

Here are some tips to help you with revision.

1. *Give yourself adequate time for revision.* As discussed above, you need time to become "cold" on your paper in order to analyze it objectively. After you have written your draft, spend some time away from it. Then try to reread it as if it had been written by someone else.

2. *Read the paper carefully.* This is tougher than it sounds. One good strategy is to read it aloud yourself or to have a friend read it aloud while you listen. (Note, however, that friends are usually not the best critics. They are rarely trained in revision techniques and are often unwilling to risk disappointing you by giving your paper a really thorough examination.)

3. *Have a list of specific items to check.* It is important to revise in an orderly fashion, in stages, looking first at large concerns, such as the overall organization, and then rereading the paper for problems with smaller elements, such as paragraph or sentence structure.

4. *Check for unity*—the clear and logical relation of all parts of the essay to its thesis. Make sure that every paragraph relates well to the whole of the paper and is in the right place.

5. *Check for coherence.* Make sure there are no gaps between the various parts of the argument. Look to see that you have adequate *transition* everywhere it is needed. Transitional elements are markers indicating places where the paper's focus or attitude changes. Transitional elements can be one word long—*however, although, unfortunately, luckily*—or as long as a sentence or a paragraph: *In order to fully appreciate the importance of stereotypes in shaping attitudes towards ethnic groups, it is necessary to examine briefly the manner in which Puerto Ricans are portrayed in popular films.*

Transitional elements rarely introduce new material. Instead, they are direction pointers, either indicating a shift to new subject matter or signaling how the writer wishes certain material to be interpreted by the reader. Because you, the writer, already know where and why your paper changes direction and how you want particular passages to be received, it can be very difficult for you to catch those places where transition is needed.

6. *Avoid unnecessary repetition.* Two types of repetition can annoy a reader: repetition of content and repetition of wording.

Repetition of content occurs when you return to a subject that you have already discussed. Ideally, you should deal with a topic once, memorably, and then move on to your next subject. Organizing a paper is a difficult task, however, that usually occurs through a process of enlightenment in terms of purposes and strategies, and repetition of content can happen even if you have used prewriting strategies. What is worse, it can be difficult for you to be aware of the repetition in your own writing. As you write and revise, remember that any unnecessary repetition of content in your final draft is potentially annoying to your readers, who are working to make sense of the argument they are reading and do not want to be distracted by a passage repeating material they have already encountered. You must train yourself, through practice, to look for material that you have repeated unnecessarily.

Repetition of wording occurs when you overuse certain phrases or words. This can make your prose sound choppy and uninspired, as the following examples demonstrate:

> The chairperson's report on the increase in psychology majors will surprise a number of people. A number of people will want copies of the report.

> The chairperson said at a press conference that she is happy with the report. She will send it to the dean in the morning. She will also make sure that the vice directors have a copy. She will send a written commendation to the committee.

> I became upset when I heard how the committee had voted. I called the chairperson and expressed my reservations about the committee's decision. I told her I felt that she had let the teachers and students of the state down. I also issued a press statement.

The last passage illustrates a condition known by composition teachers as the *I-syndrome.* Can you hear how such duplicated phrasing can hurt a paper? Your language should sound fresh and energetic. Make sure, before you submit your final draft, to read through your paper carefully, looking for such repetition. However, *not all repetition is bad.* You may wish to repeat a phrase for rhetorical effect or special emphasis: *I came. I saw. I conquered.* Just make sure that any repetition in your paper is intentional, placed there to produce a specific effect.

Editing

Editing is sometimes confused with the more involved process of revising. But editing is done later in the writing process, after you have wrestled through your first draft—and maybe your second and third—and arrived at the final draft. Even though your draft now contains all the information you want to impart and has arranged the information to your satisfaction, there are still many factors to check, such as sentence structure, spelling, and punctuation.

It is at this point that an unpracticed writer might be less than vigilant. After all, most of the work on the paper is finished, since the "big jobs" of discovering, organizing, and drafting information have been completed. *But watch out!* Editing is as important as any other part of the writing process. Any error that you allow in the final draft will count against you in the mind of the reader. This may not seem fair, but even a minor error, such as a misspelling or the confusing placement of a comma, will make a much greater impression on your reader than perhaps it should. Remember that everything about your paper is *your* responsibility, including performing even the supposedly little jobs correctly. Careless editing undermines the effectiveness of your paper. It would be a shame if all the hard work you put into prewriting, drafting, and revising were to be damaged because you carelessly allowed a comma splice!

Most of the tips given above for revising hold for editing as well. It is best to edit in stages, looking for only one or two kinds of errors each time you reread the paper. Focus especially on errors that you remember committing in the past. If, for instance, you know you have a tendency to misplace commas, go through your paper looking at each comma carefully. If you have a weakness for writing unintentional sentence fragments, read each sentence aloud to make sure that it is indeed a complete sentence. Have you accidentally shifted verb tenses anywhere, moving from past to present tense for no reason? Do all the subjects in your sentences agree in number with their verbs? *Now is the time to find out.*

Watch out for *miscues*—problems with a sentence that the writer simply does not see. Remember that your search for errors is hampered in two ways:

1. As the writer, you hope not to find any errors with your work. This desire can cause you to miss mistakes when they do occur.
2. Since you know your material so well, it is easy as you read to supply missing material—a word, a piece of punctuation—as if it were present.

How difficult is it to see that something is missing in the following sentence:

Fortunately, therapists often have sufficient regard their constituents.

We can guess that the missing word is probably *for,* which should be inserted after *regard.* It is quite possible, however, that while rereading the paper, the writer of the sentence would automatically supply the missing *for* as if it were on the page. This is a miscue, which can be hard for writers to spot because they are so close to their material.

One tactic for catching mistakes in sentence structure is to read the sentences aloud, starting with the last one in the paper and then moving to the next-to-last, then to the previous sentence, and so on, backward through the paper (reading each sentence in the normal, left-to-right manner, of course), until you reach the first sentence of the introduction. This backwards progression strips each sentence of its rhetorical context and helps you to focus on its internal structure.

Editing is the stage where you finally answer those minor questions that you had put off when you were wrestling with wording and organization. Any ambiguities regarding the use of abbreviations, italics, numerals, capital letters, titles (such as when to capitalize *director*), hyphens, dashes (usually created on a typewriter or computer by striking the hyphen key twice), apostrophes, and quotation marks have to be cleared up now. You must also check to see that you have used the required formats for footnotes, endnotes, margins, and page numbers.

Guessing is not allowed. Sometimes unpracticed writers who realize that they do not quite understand a particular rule of grammar, punctuation, or format do nothing to fill that knowledge gap. Instead they rely on guesswork and their own logic, which is not always up to the task of dealing with so contrary a language as English, to get them through problems that they could solve if they referred to a writing manual. Remember that it does not matter to the reader why or how an error shows up in your writing. It only matters that you have dropped your guard. You must not allow a careless error to undo all the good work that you have done.

Proofreading

Before you hand in your final version of the paper, it is vital that you check it one more time to make sure there are no errors of any sort. This job is called *proofreading,* or *proofing.* In essence, you are looking for many of the same things you had checked for during editing, but now you are doing it on the last draft, which is about to be submitted to your audience. Proofreading is as important as editing; you may have missed an error that you still have time to find, or an error may have been introduced when the draft was recopied or typed for the last time. Like every other stage of the writing process, proofreading is your responsibility.

At this point, you must check for such typing mistakes as transposed or deleted letters, words, phrases, or punctuation. If you have had the paper professionally typed, you still must check it carefully. Do not rely solely on the typist's proofreading. If you are creating your paper on a computer or a word processor, it is possible for you unintentionally to insert a command that alters your document drastically by slicing out a word, line, or sentence at the touch of a key. Make sure such accidental deletions have not occurred.

Above all else, remember that your paper represents *you.* It is a product of your best thinking, your most energetic and imaginative response to a writing challenge. If you have maintained your enthusiasm for the project and worked through the stages of the writing process honestly and carefully, you should produce a paper you can be proud of, one that will serve its readers well.

2 Writing Competently

2.1 Grammar and Style

The Competent Writer

Good writing places your thoughts in your readers' minds in exactly the way you want them to be there. Good writing tells your readers just what you want them to know without telling them anything you do not want them to know. This may sound odd, but the fact is writers have to be careful not to let unwanted messages slip into their writing. Look, for example, at the passage below, taken from a paper analyzing the impact of a worker-retraining program. Hidden within the prose is a message that jeopardizes the paper's success. Can you detect the message?

> Recent articles written on the subject of recovered memories have had little to say about the particular problems dealt with in this paper. Since few of these articles focus on the problem in depth.

Chances are, when you reached the end of the second "sentence," you felt that something was missing and perceived a gap in logic or coherence, so you went back through both sentences to find the place where things had gone wrong. The second sentence is actually not a sentence at all. It does have certain features of a sentence—for example, a subject (*few*) and a verb (*focus*)—but its first word (*Since*) subordinates the entire clause that follows, taking away its ability to stand on its own as a complete idea. The second "sentence," which is properly called a *subordinate clause*, merely fills in some information about the first sentence, telling us why recent articles about dislocated workers fail to deal with problems discussed in the present paper.

The sort of error represented by the second "sentence" is commonly called a *sentence fragment,* and it conveys to the reader a message that no writer wants to send: that the writer either is careless or—worse—has not mastered the language. Language errors such as fragments, misplaced commas, or shifts in verb tense send out warnings in the readers' minds. As a result the readers lose some of their concentration on the issue being discussed; they become distracted and begin to wonder about the language competency of the writer. The writing loses effectiveness.

NOTE. Whatever goal you set for your paper—to persuade, describe, analyze, or speculate—you must also set one other goal: *to display language competence.* If your paper does not meet this goal, it will not completely achieve its other aims. Language errors spread doubt like a virus; they jeopardize all the hard work you have done on your paper. Anyone who doubts that language competence is essential for establishing credibility should remember the beating that Vice President Dan Quayle took in the press for misspelling the word *potato* at a spelling bee in 1992. His error caused a storm of humiliating publicity for the hapless Quayle, adding to an impression of his general incompetence.

Correctness Is Relative

Although they may seem minor, the sort of language errors we are discussing—often called *surface errors*—can be extremely damaging in certain kinds of writing. Surface errors come in a variety of types, including misspellings, punctuation problems, grammar errors, and the inconsistent use of abbreviations, capitalization, and numerals. These errors are an affront to your readers' notion of correctness, and therein lies one of the biggest problems with surface errors. Different audiences tolerate different levels of correctness. You know that you can get away with surface errors in, say, a letter to a friend, who will probably not judge you harshly for them, while those same errors in a job application letter might eliminate you from consideration for the position. Correctness depends to an extent upon context.

Another problem is that the rules governing correctness shift over time. What would have been an error to your grandmother's generation—the splitting of an infinitive, for example, or the ending of a sentence with a preposition—is taken in stride today by most readers.

So how do you write correctly when the rules shift from person to person and over time? Here are some tips.

Consider Your Audience

One of the great risks of writing is that even the simplest of choices regarding wording or punctuation can sometimes prejudice your audience against you in ways that may seem unfair. For example, look again at the old grammar rule forbidding the splitting of infinitives. After decades of telling students to *never* split an infinitive (something just done in this sentence), composition experts now concede that a split infinitive is *not* a grammar crime. But suppose you have written a position paper trying to convince your city research committee of the need to hire security personnel for the library, and half of the research committee members—the people you wish to convince—remember their eighth-grade grammar teacher's warning about splitting infinitives. How will they respond when you tell them, in your introduction, that librarians are compelled "to always accompany" visitors to the rare book room because of the threat of vandalism? How much of their attention have you suddenly lost because of their automatic recollection of what is now a nonrule? It is possible, in other words, to write correctly and still offend your readers' notions of language competence.

Make sure that you tailor the surface features and the degree of formality of your writing to the level of competency that your readers require. When in doubt, take a conservative approach. Your audience might be just as distracted by contractions as by a split infinitive.

Aim for Consistency

When dealing with a language question for which there are different answers—such as whether to use a comma before the conjunction in a series of three ("The chairperson's lecture addressed *taxes, housing for the poor,* and *the job situation.*")—always use the same strategy throughout your paper. If, for example, you avoid splitting one infinitive, avoid splitting *all* infinitives.

Have Confidence in What You Know About Writing!

It is easy for unpracticed writers to allow their occasional mistakes to shake their confidence in their writing ability. The fact is, however, that most of what we know about writing is correct. We are all capable, for example, of writing grammatically sound phrases, even if we cannot list the rules by which we achieve coherence. Most writers who worry about their chronic errors make fewer mistakes than they think. Becoming distressed about errors makes writing even more difficult.

Grammar

As various composition theorists have pointed out, the word *grammar* has several definitions. One meaning is "the formal patterns in which words must be arranged in order to convey meaning." We learn these patterns very early in life and use them spontaneously, without thinking. Our understanding of grammatical patterns is extremely sophisticated, despite the fact that few of us can actually cite the rules by which the patterns work. Patrick Hartwell (1985, p. 111) tested grammar learning by asking native English speakers of different ages and levels of education, including high school teachers, to arrange these words in natural order:

French   young   the   girls   four

Everyone could produce the natural order for this phrase: "the four young French girls." Yet none of Hartwell's respondents said they knew the rule that governs the order of the words.

Eliminate Chronic Errors

But if just thinking about our errors has a negative effect on our writing, how do we learn to write more correctly? Perhaps the best answer is simply to write as often as possible. Give yourself lots of practice in putting your thoughts into written shape—and then in revising and proofing your work. As you write and revise, be honest with yourself, and patient. Chronic errors are like bad habits; getting rid of them takes time.

You probably know of one or two problem areas in your writing that you could have eliminated but have not done so. Instead you have "fudged" your writing at the critical points, relying upon half-remembered formulas from past English classes or trying to come up with logical solutions to your writing problems.

WARNING. The English language does not always work in a way that seems logical. You may have simply decided that comma rules are unlearnable or that you will never understand the difference between the verbs *lay* and *lie*. And so you guess and come up with the wrong answer a good part of the time. What a shame, when just a little extra work would give you mastery over those few gaps in your understanding and boost your confidence as well.

Instead of continuing with this sort of guesswork and living with the gaps in your knowledge, why not face the problem areas now and learn the rules that have heretofore escaped you? What follows is a discussion of those surface features of writing where errors most commonly occur. You will probably be familiar with most if not all of the rules discussed, but there may well be a few you have not yet mastered. Now is the time to do so.

2.2 Fixing Common Errors

Apostrophes

An apostrophe is used to show possession; when you wish to say that something belongs to someone or something, you add either an apostrophe and an *s* or an apostrophe alone to the word that represents the owner.

When the owner is *singular* (a single person or thing), the apostrophe precedes an added *s:*

According to Dr. Anderson's secretary, the therapy session has been canceled.

The client's lawyers challenged the therapist's competency in court.

Somebody's briefcase was left in the classroom.

The same rule applies if the word showing possession is a plural that does not end in *s:*

The women's club sponsored several informational sessions on date rape.

Dr. Smith has proven himself a tireless worker for children's rights.

When the word expressing ownership is a *plural* ending in *s,* the apostrophe follows the *s:*

The new policy was discussed at the secretaries' conference.

There are two ways to form the possessive for two or more nouns:

1. To show joint possession (both nouns owning the same thing or things), the last noun in the series is possessive:

   The director and first lady's invitations were sent out yesterday.

2. To indicate that each noun owns an item or items individually, each noun must show possession:

   Dr. Scott's and Dr. MacKay's treatment plans took different approaches to the same problem.

The importance of the apostrophe is obvious when you consider the difference in meaning between the following two sentences:

Be sure to pick up the professor's bags on your way to the airport.

Be sure to pick up the professors' bags on your way to the airport.

In the first sentence, you have only one professor to worry about, while in the second, you have at least two!

Capitalization

Here is a brief summary of some hard-to-remember capitalization rules:

1. You may, if you choose, capitalize the first letter of the first word in a complete sentence that follows a colon. However, make sure you use one pattern consistently throughout your paper:

   Our instructions are explicit: *Do* not allow anyone into the adolescent development conference without an identification badge.

   Our instructions are explicit: *do* not allow anyone into the adolescent development conference without an identification badge.

2. Capitalize *proper nouns* (names of specific people, places, or things) and *proper adjectives* (adjectives made from proper nouns). A common noun following a proper adjective is usually not capitalized, nor is a common adjective preceding a proper adjective (such as *a, an,* or *the*):

PROPER NOUNS	PROPER ADJECTIVES
Adler	Adlerian therapy
American Psychological Association	the APA convention
Freud	a Freudian theory

Proper nouns include:

Names of monuments and buildings: the Washington Monument, the Empire State Building, the Library of Congress

Historical events, eras, and certain terms concerning calendar dates: the Civil War, the Dark Ages, Monday, December, Columbus Day

Parts of the country: North, Southwest, Eastern Seaboard, the West Coast, New England.

NOTE. When words like *north, south, east, west, northwest* are used to designate direction rather than geographical region, they are not capitalized: "We drove *east* to Boston and then made a tour of the East Coast."

Words referring to race, religion, and nationality: Islam, Muslim, Caucasian, White (*or* white), Asian, Negro, Black (*or* black), Slavic, Arab, Jewish, Hebrew, Buddhism, Buddhists, Southern Baptists, the Bible, the Koran, American

Names of languages: English, Chinese, Latin, Sanskrit

Titles of corporations, institutions, universities, and organizations: Dow Chemical, General Motors, the National Endowment for the Humanities, University of Tennessee, Colby College, Kiwanis Club, American Association of Retired Persons, Oklahoma State Senate

NOTE. Some words once considered proper nouns or adjectives have, over time, become common, such as *french fries, pasteurized milk, arabic numerals, italics.*

3. Titles of individuals may be capitalized if they precede a proper name; otherwise, titles are usually not capitalized.

The committee honored Director Seligman.

The committee honored the newly elected director.

We phoned Doctor Jessup, who arrived shortly afterward.

We phoned the doctor, who arrived shortly afterward.

A story on President Bush's health appeared in yesterday's paper.

A story on the president's health appeared in yesterday's paper.

When Not to Capitalize

In general, you do not capitalize nouns when your reference is nonspecific. For example, you would not capitalize *the mayor*, but you would capitalize *Mayor Smith*. The second reference is as much a title as it is a term of identification, while the first reference is a mere identifier. Likewise, there is a difference in degree of specificity between *the psychology department* and *the Department of Psychology at the University of Southern Maine*.

Capitalization depends to some extent on the context of your writing. For example, if you are writing an analysis for a specific corporation, you may capitalize words and phrases that refer to that corporation—such as *Board of Directors*, *Chairman of the Board*, and *the Institute*—that would not be capitalized in a paper written for a more general audience. Likewise, in some contexts it is not unusual to see the titles of certain powerful officials capitalized even when not accompanying a proper noun:

> The President took only a few members of his staff with him to the conference.

Colons

We all know certain uses for the colon. A colon can, for example, separate the parts of a statement of time (4:25 A.M.), separate chapter and verse in a biblical quotation (John 3:16), and close the salutation of a business letter (Dear Dr. Keaton:). But the colon has other, less well known uses that can add extra flexibility to sentence structure.

The colon can introduce into a sentence certain kinds of material, such as a list, a quotation, or a restatement or description of material mentioned earlier:

LIST

The therapist's report promised to do three things: (1) establish the extent of the problem; (2) examine several possible treatment options; and (3) estimate the advantages and disadvantages of each treatment option.

QUOTATION

In his lecture, the director challenged us with these words: "How will your work make a difference in the life of your client?"

RESTATEMENT OR DESCRIPTION

Ahead of us, according to the director, lay the biggest job of all: convincing our clients of the plan's benefits.

Commas

The comma is perhaps the most troublesome of all marks of punctuation, no doubt because its use is governed by so many variables, such as sentence length, rhetorical emphasis, and changing notions of style. The most common problems are outlined below.

The Comma Splice

A *comma splice* is the joining of two complete sentences with only a comma:

An initial interview merely provides a possible diagnosis, determining the actual diagnosis usually requires further investigation of the body.

An unemployed worker faces many emotional challenges, he must first face his image of himself.

It might be possible for the therapist to delay treatment, however, such a move would be criticized by her colleagues.

In each of these above passages, two complete sentences (also called *independent clauses*) have been spliced together by a comma, which is an inadequate break between the two sentences.

One foolproof way to check your paper for comma splices is to read carefully the structures on both sides of each comma. If you find a complete sentence on each side, and if the sentence following the comma does not begin with a coordinating conjunction (*and, but, for, nor, or, so, yet*), then you have found a comma splice.

Simply reading the draft to try to "hear" the comma splices may not work, since the rhetorical features of your prose—its "movement"—may make it hard to detect this kind of error in sentence completeness. There are five commonly used ways to correct comma splices:

1. Place a period between the two independent clauses:

    INCORRECT: A doctoral candidate finds many challenges in writing her dissertation, she finds opportunities as well.

    CORRECT: A doctoral candidate finds many challenges in writing her dissertation. There are opportunities as well.

2. Place a comma and a coordinating conjunction (*and, but, for, or, nor, so, yet*) between the sentences:

    INCORRECT: The student's presentation described the major differences of opinion over recovered memories, it also suggested areas for future research.

CORRECT: The student's presentation described the major differences of opinion over recovered memories, *and* it also suggested areas for future research.

3. Place a semicolon between the independent clauses:

INCORRECT: Some students feel that the department should provide a student lounge, many others disagree.

CORRECT: Some students feel that the department should provide a student lounge; many others disagree.

4. Rewrite the two clauses as one independent clause:

INCORRECT: Planning played a big part in the treatment process, however, it was not the deciding factor in the treatment's success.

CORRECT: Planning played a big but not decisive part in the treatment process.

5. Change one of the independent clauses into a dependent clause by beginning it with a *subordinating word* (for example, *although, after, as, because, before, if, though, unless, when, which, where*), which prevents the clause from being able to stand on its own as a complete sentence.

INCORRECT: The meeting was held last Tuesday, there was a poor turnout.

CORRECT: When the meeting was held last Tuesday, there was poor turnout.

Commas in a Compound Sentence

A *compound sentence* is comprised of two or more independent clauses—two complete sentences. When these two clauses are joined by a coordinating conjunction, the conjunction should be preceded by a comma to signal the reader that another independent clause follows. (This is method number 2 for fixing a comma splice described above.) When the comma is missing, the reader is not expecting to find the second half of a compound sentence and may be distracted from the text.

As the following examples indicate, the missing comma is especially a problem in longer sentences or in sentences in which other coordinating conjunctions appear. Notice how the comma sorts out the two main parts of the compound sentence, eliminating confusion:

INCORRECT: The director promised to visit the hospital and investigate the problem and then he called the meeting to a close.

CORRECT: The director promised to visit the hospital and investigate the problem, and then he called the meeting to a close.

INCORRECT: The coordinating committee can neither make policy nor enforce it nor can its members serve on auxiliary committees.

CORRECT: The coordinating committee can neither make policy nor en-
                  force it, nor can its members serve on auxiliary committees.

An exception to this rule arises in shorter sentences, where the comma may not be necessary to make the meaning clear:

The psychiatrist phoned and we thanked him for his opinion.

However, it is never wrong to place a comma after the conjunction between the independent clauses. If you are the least bit unsure of your audience's notion of "proper" grammar, it is a good idea to take the conservative approach and use the comma:

The psychiatrist phoned, and we thanked him for his opinion.

Commas with Restrictive and Nonrestrictive Elements

A *nonrestrictive element* is a part of a sentence—a word, phrase, or clause— that adds information about another element in the sentence without restricting or limiting its meaning. While its information may be useful, the nonrestrictive element is not needed for the sentence to make sense. To signal its inessential nature, the nonrestrictive element is set off from the rest of the sentence with commas.

The failure to use commas to indicate the nonrestrictive nature of a sentence element can cause confusion. See, for example, how the presence or absence of commas affects our understanding of the following sentence:

The chairperson was talking with the student, who won the outstanding service award last year.

The chairperson was talking with the student who won the outstanding service award last year.

Can you see that the comma changes the meaning of the sentence? In the first version of the sentence, the comma makes the information that follows it incidental:

The chairperson was talking with the student, who happens to have won the service award last year.

In the second version of the sentence, the information following the word *student* is vital to the sense of the sentence; it tells us specifically *which* student— presumably there are more than one—the chairperson was addressing. Here the lack of a comma has transformed the material following the word *student* into a *restrictive element*, which means that it is necessary to our understanding of the sentence.

Be sure that in your paper you make a clear distinction between nonrestrictive and restrictive elements by setting off the nonrestrictive elements with commas.

Commas in a Series

A *series* is any two or more items of a similar nature that appear consecutively in a sentence. These items may be individual words, phrases, or clauses. In a series of three or more items, the items are separated by commas:

> *The research director, the project manager,* and *the technician* all attended the briefing. Because of the new safety regulations, *testing equipment must be moved out of the office, technicians must apply for recertification,* and *examination schedules must be reviewed.*

The final comma in the series, the one before *and*, is sometimes left out, especially in newspaper writing. This practice, however, can make for confusion, especially in longer, complicated sentences like the second example above. Here is the way this sentence would read without the final, or *serial*, comma:

> Because of the new safety regulations, testing equipment must be moved out of the office, technicians must apply for recertification and examination schedules must be reviewed.

Notice that without a comma the division between the second and third items in the series is not clear. This is the sort of ambiguous structure that can cause a reader to backtrack and lose concentration. You can avoid such confusion by always using that final comma. Remember, however, that if you do decide to include it, do so consistently; make sure it appears in every series in your paper.

Dangling Modifiers

A *modifier* is a word or group of words used to describe, or modify, another word in the sentence. A *dangling modifier* appears at either the beginning or end of a sentence and seems to be describing some word other than the one the writer obviously intended. The modifier therefore "dangles," disconnected from its correct meaning. It is often hard for the writer to spot a dangling modifier, but readers can—and will—find them, and the result can be disastrous for the sentence, as the following examples demonstrate:

INCORRECT:	*Driving by the office,* the receptionist was seen.
CORRECT:	*Driving by the office,* we saw the receptionist.
INCORRECT:	*Worried at the cost of the program,* sections of the program were trimmed in committee.
CORRECT:	*Worried at the cost of the program,* the committee trimmed sections of the program.
INCORRECT:	*To promote reform,* a lot of effort went into the television ads.
CORRECT:	The committee put a lot of effort into the television ads advocating reform.

INCORRECT: *Stunned,* the television broadcast the director's explanation.

CORRECT: The television broadcast the stunned director's explanation.

Note that in the first two incorrect sentences above, the confusion is largely due to the use of *passive-voice verbs:* "the office *was seen,*" "sections of the program *were trimmed.*" Often, although not always, a dangling modifier results because the actor in the sentence—*we* in the first sentence, *the committee* in the second—is either distanced from the modifier or obliterated by the passive-voice verb. It is a good idea to avoid using the passive voice unless you have a specific reason for doing so.

One way to check for dangling modifiers is to examine all modifiers at the beginning or end of your sentences. Look especially for *to be* phrases or for words ending in *-ing* or *-ed* at the start of the modifier. Then see if the modified word is close enough to the phrase to be properly connected.

Parallelism

Series of two or more words, phrases, or clauses within a sentence should have the same grammatical structure. This pattern is called *parallelism.* Parallel structures can add power and balance to your writing by creating a strong rhetorical rhythm. Here is a famous example of parallelism from the Preamble to the U.S. Constitution. (The capitalization follows that of the original eighteenth-century document. Parallel structures have been italicized.)

> We the People of the United States, in Order to *form a more perfect Union, Establish justice, insure Domestic Tranquillity, provide for the common defense, promote the general Welfare, and secure the Blessings of Liberty to ourselves and our Posterity,* do *ordain* and *establish* this Constitution for the United States of America.

There are actually two series in this sentence, the first composed of six phrases that each complete the infinitive phrase beginning with the word *to* (*to form, [to] Establish, [to] ensure, [to] provide, [to] promote, [to] secure*), the second consisting of two verbs (*ordain* and *establish*). These parallel series appeal to our love of balance and pattern, and they give an authoritative tone to the sentence. The writer, we feel, has thought long and carefully about the matter at hand and has taken firm control of it.

Because we find a special satisfaction in balanced structures, we are more likely to remember ideas phrased in parallelisms than in less highly ordered language. For this reason, as well as for the sense of authority and control that they suggest, parallel structures are common in civic utterances:

> But in a larger sense, we cannot dedicate—we cannot consecrate—we cannot hallow—this ground. The brave men, living and dead, who struggled here, have consecrated it far above our poor power to add or detract. The world will little note, nor long remember what we say here; but it can never forget what they did here.
>
>   Abraham Lincoln, Gettysburg Address, 1863

Faulty Parallelism

If the parallelism of a passage is not carefully maintained, the writing can seem sloppy and out of balance. Scan your writing to make sure that all series and lists have parallel structure. The following examples show how to correct faulty parallelism:

INCORRECT: The chairperson promises not only *to reform* the psychology department but also *the giving of raises* to all city employees. [Connective structures such as *not only . . . but also*, and *both . . . and* introduce elements that should be parallel.]

CORRECT: The chairperson promises not only *to reform* the psychology department but also *to give raises* to all department employees.

INCORRECT: Here are the items on the committee's agenda: (1) *to discuss* the new project costs; (2) *to revise* the wording of the report; (3) *a vote* on the budget.

CORRECT: Here are the items on the committee's agenda: (1) *to discuss* the new project costs; (2) *to revise* the wording of the report; (3) *to vote* on the budget.

Fused (Run-On) Sentences

A *fused sentence* is one in which two or more independent clauses (passages that can stand as complete sentences) have been run together without the aid of any suitable connecting word, phrase, or punctuation. There are several ways to correct a fused sentence:

INCORRECT: The research committee members were exhausted they had debated for two hours.

CORRECT: The research committee members were exhausted. They had debated for two hours. [The clauses have been separated into two sentences.]

CORRECT: The research committee members were exhausted; they had debated for two hours. [The clauses have been separated by a semicolon.]

CORRECT: The research committee members were exhausted, having debated for two hours. [The second clause has been changed to a participial phrase describing the condition of the committee members in the preceding independent clause.]

INCORRECT: Our analysis impressed the committee it also convinced them to reconsider their action.

CORRECT: Our analysis impressed the committee and also convinced them to reconsider their action. [The second clause has been reworded as part of the first clause.]

CORRECT: Our analysis impressed the committee, and it also convinced
                  them to reconsider their action. [The independent clauses
                  have been separated by a comma and a coordinating word.]

While a fused sentence is easily noticeable to the reader, it can be madden-ingly difficult for the writer to catch. Unpracticed writers tend to read through the fused spots, unconsciously supplying the break that is usually heard when sentences are spoken. To check for fused sentences, read the independent clauses in your paper *carefully*, making sure that there are adequate breaks among all of them.

Pronoun Errors

Its Versus *It's*

Do not make the mistake of trying to form the possessive of *it* in the same way that you form the possessive of most nouns. The pronoun *it* shows posses-sion by simply adding an *s*.

The research director argued the case on *its* merits.

The word *it's* is a contraction, meaning *it is:*

It's the most expensive program ever launched by the research committee.

What makes the *its/it's* rule so confusing is that most nouns form the singu-lar possessive by adding an apostrophe and an *s:*

The *committee's* decision startled the director.

When proofreading, any time you come to the word *it's*, substitute the phrase *it is* while you read. If the phrase makes sense, you have used the correct form. If you have used the word *it's:*

The research article was misleading in *it's* analysis of the group's behavior.

then read it as *it is:*

The research report was misleading in *it is* analysis of the group's
behavior.

If the phrase makes no sense, substitute *its* for *it's:*

The research report was misleading in *its* analysis of the group's behavior.

Vague Pronoun References

Pronouns are words that take the place of nouns or other pronouns that have already been mentioned in your writing. The most common pronouns in-clude *he, she, it, they, them, those, which,* and *who.* You must make sure that there is no confusion about the word to which each pronoun refers:

The chairperson said that *he* would support our bill if the city research committee would also back it.

The word that the pronoun replaces is called its *antecedent.* To check the accuracy of your pronoun references, ask yourself, "To what does the pronoun refer?" Then answer the question carefully, making sure that there is not more than one possible antecedent. Consider the following example:

Several special interest groups decided to defeat the new health service provider licensing bill. *This* became the turning point of the government's reform interview.

To what does the word *This* refer? The immediate answer seems to be the word *bill* at the end of the previous sentence. It is more likely that the writer was referring to the attempt of the special interest groups to defeat the bill, but there is no word in the first sentence that refers specifically to this action. The pronoun reference is thus unclear. One way to clarify the reference is to change the beginning of the second sentence:

Several special interest groups decided to defeat the new health service provider licensing bill. *Their attack on the bill* became the turning point of the government's reform interview.

This point is further demonstrated by the following sentence:

When the hospital administrator appointed his brother John to the position of special investigator, *he* had little idea how widespread the corruption in the Teamsters Hospital was.

To whom does the word *he* refer? It is unclear whether the writer is referring to the administrator or his brother. One way to clarify the reference is simply to repeat the antecedent instead of using a pronoun:

When the hospital administrator appointed his brother John to the position of special investigator, *the administrator* had little idea how widespread the corruption in the Teamsters Hospital was.

Pronoun Agreement

A pronoun must agree with its antecedent in both gender and number, as the following examples demonstrate:

Chairperson Smith said that *he* appreciated our club's support in the election.

One staff member asked the nurse what *she* would do if the administrator offered *her* an administrative position.

Having listened to our case, the arbitrator decided to rule on *it* within the week.

Therapists working with the client said *they* were pleased with the progress so far.

Certain words, however, can be troublesome antecedents, because they may look like plural pronouns but are actually singular:

anyone	everybody	no one
each	everyone	somebody
either	nobody	someone

A pronoun referring to one of these words in a sentence must be singular too.

INCORRECT: *Each* of the women in the support group brought *their* children.

CORRECT: *Each* of the women in the support group brought *her* children.

INCORRECT: Has *everybody* received *their* schedule?

CORRECT: Has *everybody* received *his or her* schedule? [The two gender specific pronouns are used to avoid sexist language.]

CORRECT: Have *all the delegates* received *their* schedules? [The singular antecedent has been changed to a plural one.]

A Shift in Person

It is important to avoid shifting unnecessarily among first person (*I, we*), second person (*you*), and third person (*she, he, it, one, they*). Such shifts can cause confusion:

INCORRECT: *Most people* [third person] who apply for a promotion find that if *you* [second person] tell the truth during *your* interview, *you* will gain the director's respect.

CORRECT: *Most people* who apply for a promotion find that if *they* tell the truth during *their* interviews, *they* will gain the director's respect.

INCORRECT: *One* [first person] cannot tell whether *they* [third person] are suited for being a therapist until *they* decide to try.

CORRECT: *One* cannot tell whether *one* is suited for being a therapist until *one* decides to try.

Quotation Marks

It can be difficult to remember when to use quotation marks and where they go in relation to other punctuation. When faced with these questions, unpracticed writers often try to rely on logic rather than on a rule book, but the rules do not always seem to rely on logic. The only way to make sure of your use of quotation marks is to *memorize* the rules. Luckily, there are not many.

The Use of Quotation Marks

Use quotation marks to enclose direct quotations that are not longer than four typed lines:

> The chairperson said that he would "keep the committee in session until it came to a decision."

Longer quotes are placed in a double-spaced block, *without* quotation marks:

> At one point the patient's narrative took an odd turn:

> > John Jacob Jingleheimer Schmidt was a good old boy. I mean he was simply no good as a therapist. One day he told me to go jump in a lake, I was up to my ears in barbecued catfish already. I mean, go figure! A guy with a reputation like that has got to be a preacher's kid or something. (Castle, 1989, p. 45)

Use single quotation marks to set off quotations within quotations:

> "I intend," said the director, "to use in my proposal a line from Frost's poem, 'The Road Not Taken.'"

NOTE. When the quote occurs at the end of the sentence, both the single and double quotation marks are placed outside the period.

Use quotation marks to set off titles of the following:

> short poems (those not printed as a separate volume) and short stories
> articles or essays
> songs
> episodes of television or radio shows

Use quotation marks to set off words or phrases used in special ways:

1. To convey irony:

> The "therapeutic" plan has done nothing but increase my distress.

2. To indicate a technical term:

> "White matter" consists of axon bundles that carry messages to and from the brain. This study will illustrate certain characteristics of white matter. [Once the term is defined, it is not placed in quotation marks again.]

Quotation Marks in Relation to Other Punctuation

Place commas and periods *inside* closing quotation marks:

> "My fellow psychologists," said the chairperson, "there are tough times ahead of us."

Place colons and semicolons *outside* closing quotation marks:

> In his lecture on techniques, the chairperson warned against "an encroaching indolence"; he was referring to the freshman class.

Three types of victims were identified in the booklet entitled "Five Steps to Reclamation": the perpetrator, the abused, and the families of all concerned.

Use the context to determine whether to place question marks, exclamation points, and dashes inside or outside closing quotation marks. If the punctuation is part of the quotation, place it *inside* the quotation mark:

"When will the committee make up its mind?" asked the applicant.

The patient shouted, "Free the hostages!" and "No more slavery!"

If the punctuation is not part of the quotation, place it *outside* the quotation mark:

Which substance abuse counselor said, "We have nothing to fear but beer itself"? [Although the quote is a complete sentence, you do not place a period after it. There can only be one piece of terminal punctuation, or punctuation that ends a sentence.]

Semicolons

The semicolon is a little-used punctuation mark that you should learn to incorporate into your writing strategy because of its many potential applications. For example, a semicolon can be used to correct a comma splice:

INCORRECT: The hospital representatives left the meeting in good spirits, their demands were met.

CORRECT: The hospital representatives left the meeting in good spirits; their demands were met.

INCORRECT: Several guests at the fundraiser had lost their invitations, however, we were able to seat them anyway.

CORRECT: Several guests at the fundraiser had lost their invitations; however, we were able to seat them anyway. [Conjunctive adverbs like *however, therefore*, and *thus* are not coordinating words (such as *and, but, or, for, so, yet*) and cannot be used with a comma to link independent clauses. If the second independent clause begins with *however*, it must be preceded by either a period or a semicolon.]

As you can see from the second example above, connecting two independent clauses with a semicolon instead of a period strengthens their relationship.

Semicolons can also separate items in a series when the series items themselves contain commas:

The college newspaper account of the department meeting stressed the food fight, which drew the biggest crowd; the chairperson's lecture, which drew Bronx cheers; and the party in the park, which lasted for hours.

Avoid misusing semicolons. For example, use a comma, not a semicolon, to separate an independent clause from a dependent clause:

INCORRECT: Students from the college volunteered to answer phones during the pledge drive; which was set up to generate money for the new treatment center.

CORRECT: Students from the college volunteered to answer phones during the pledge drive, which was set up to generate money for the new treatment center.

Do not overuse semicolons. Although they are useful, too many semicolons in your writing can distract your readers' attention. Avoid monotony by using semicolons sparingly.

Sentence Fragments

A fragment is an incomplete part of a sentence that is punctuated and capitalized as if it were an entire sentence. It is an especially disruptive error, because it obscures the connections that the words of a sentence must make in order to complete the reader's understanding.

Students sometimes write fragments because they are concerned that a sentence needs to be shortened. Remember that cutting the length of a sentence merely by adding a period somewhere often creates a fragment. When checking your writing for fragments, it is essential that you read each sentence carefully to determine whether it has: (1) a complete subject and a verb and (2) a subordinating word before the subject and verb, which makes the construction a subordinate clause rather than a complete sentence.

Types of Sentence Fragments

Some fragments lack a verb:

INCORRECT: The chairperson of our committee, having received a letter from the director. [The word *having*, which can be used as a verb, is here being used as a present participle introducing a participial phrase. Watch out for words that look like verbs but are being used in another way.]

CORRECT: The chairperson of our committee received a letter from the director.

Some fragments lack a subject:

INCORRECT: Our study shows that there is broad support for improvement in the mental health care system. And in the insurance system.

CORRECT: Our study shows that there is broad support for improvement in the mental health care system and in the insurance system.

Some fragments are subordinate clauses:

INCORRECT: After the latest edition of the departmental newspaper came out. [This clause has the two major components of a complete sentence: a subject (*edition*) and a verb (*came*). Indeed, if the first word (*After*) were deleted, the clause would be a complete sentence. But that first word is a *subordinating word*, which prevents the following clause from standing on its own as a complete sentence. Watch out for this kind of construction. It is called a *subordinate clause*, and it is not a sentence.]

CORRECT: After the latest edition of the departmental newspaper came out, the chairperson's secretary was overwhelmed with phone calls. [A common method of correcting a subordinate clause that has been punctuated as a complete sentence is to connect it to the complete sentence to which it is closest in meaning.]

INCORRECT: Several representatives asked for copies of the director's position paper. Which called for reform of the agency.

CORRECT: Several representatives asked for copies of the director's position paper, which called for reform of the agency.

Spelling

All of us have problems spelling certain words that we have not yet committed to memory. But most writers are not as bad at spelling as they believe they are. Usually it is a handful of words that an individual finds troubling. It is important to be as sensitive as possible to your own particular spelling problems—and to keep a dictionary handy. There is no excuse for failing to check spelling.

What follows are a list of commonly confused words and a list of commonly misspelled words. Read through the lists, looking for those words that tend to give you trouble. If you have any questions, *consult your dictionary*.

COMMONLY CONFUSED WORDS

accept/except	ascent/assent	cite/sight/site
advice/advise	bare/bear	complement/
affect/effect	brake/break	compliment
aisle/isle	breath/breathe	conscience/conscious
allusion/illusion	buy/by	corps/corpse
an/and	capital/capitol	council/counsel
angel/angle	choose/chose	dairy/diary

descent/dissent

desert/dessert

device/devise

die/dye

dominant/dominate

elicit/illicit

eminent/immanent/
   imminent

envelop/envelope

every day/everyday

fair/fare

formally/formerly

forth/fourth

hear/here

heard/herd

hole/whole

human/humane

its/it's

know/no

later/latter

lay/lie

lead/led

lessen/lesson

loose/lose

may be/maybe

miner/minor

moral/morale

of/off

passed/past

patience/patients

peace/piece

personal/personnel

plain/plane

precede/proceed

presence/presents

principal/principle

quiet/quite

rain/reign/rein

raise/raze

reality/realty

respectfully/respectively

reverend/reverent

right/rite/write

road/rode

scene/seen

sense/since

stationary/stationery

straight/strait

taught/taut

than/then

their/there/they're

threw/through

too/to/two

track/tract

waist/waste

waive/wave

weak/week

weather/whether

were/where

which/witch

whose/who's

your/you're

COMMONLY MISSPELLED WORDS

a lot

acceptable

accessible

accommodate

accompany

accustomed

acquire

against

annihilate

apparent

arguing

argument

authentic

before

begin

beginning

believe

benefited

bulletin

business

cannot

category

committee

condemn

courteous

definitely

dependent

desperate

develop

different

disappear

disappoint

easily

efficient

environment

equipped

exceed

exercise

existence

experience

fascinate

finally

foresee

forty

fulfill

gauge

guaranteed

guard

harass

hero

heroes

humorous

hurried

hurriedly

hypocrite

ideally

immediately	occurrences	recommend	succeed
immense	omission	referring	success
incredible	omit	religious	successfully
innocuous	opinion	remembrance	susceptible
intercede	opponent	reminisce	suspicious
interrupt	parallel	repetition	technical
irrelevant	parole	representative	temporary
irresistible	peaceable	rhythm	tendency
irritate	performance	ridiculous	therefore
knowledge	pertain	roommate	tragedy
license	practical	satellite	truly
likelihood	preparation	scarcity	tyranny
maintenance	probably	scenery	unanimous
manageable	process	science	unconscious
meanness	professor	secede	undoubtedly
mischievous	prominent	secession	until
missile	pronunciation	secretary	vacuum
necessary	psychology	senseless	valuable
nevertheless	publicly	separate	various
no one	pursue	sergeant	vegetable
noticeable	pursuing	shining	visible
noticing	questionnaire	significant	without
nuisance	realize	sincerely	women
occasion	receipt	skiing	writing
occasionally	received	stubbornness	
occurred	recession	studying	

3

Student Paper Formats in APA Style

Your format makes your paper's first impression. Justly or not, accurately or not, it announces your professional competence—or lack of competence. A well-executed format implies that your paper is worth reading. More importantly, however, a proper format brings information to your readers in a familiar form that has the effect of setting their minds at ease. Your paper's format should therefore impress your readers with your academic competence as a psychologist by following accepted professional standards. Like the style and clarity of your writing, your format communicates messages that are often more readily and profoundly received than the content of the document itself.

This chapter provides instructions for formatting the following elements of a psychology paper:

General page format	Text
Title page	Chapter headings
Abstract	Tables, illustrations, and figures
Table of contents	References
Lists of tables and figures	Appendix

NOTE. In general, the paper format described in this chapter is taken from instructions published in the fourth edition of the *Publication Manual of the American Psychological Association* (1994). But the APA *Manual* (p. 331) explains that its primary function is to serve as a guide to the preparation of manuscripts for publication in journals. The *Manual* (pp. 331–332) notes that, for a variety of reasons, there may be distinctions between the format for a paper written to be published and the format for an academic paper, such as a thesis, dissertation, or class paper. While noting that the professional format it describes may work well in an academic setting, the APA *Manual* (p. 332) <u>advises that student writers make sure the format they use satisfies requirements set by their individual institutions.</u>

The format instructions that follow are based on the standard APA format for professional papers. When the APA *Manual* suggest an alternate format decision for student papers, that alternate is included and clearly designated, as are suggestions that are not found in the APA *Manual* but that are, instead, recommended by the writers of this manual.

3.1 General Page Format

Psychology assignments should be typed or printed on 8 1/2-by-11-inch premium white bond paper, 20 pound or heavier. Do not use any other color or size except to comply with special instructions from your instructor, and do not use an off-white or poor quality (draft) paper. Psychology that is worth the time to write and read is worth good paper.

Always submit to your instructor an original typed or computer-printed (preferably laser-printed) manuscript. While the APA *Manual* (1994, p. 335) observes that most universities will allow you to submit a photocopy of your paper, the writers of this manual suggest that, if possible, you should submit an original, always remembering to make a second copy for your own files in case the original is lost.

Margins, according to the APA *Manual* (1994, p. 240), should be one inch on all sides of the paper. However, the APA *Manual* (p. 335) also notes that, if you are preparing a college thesis or dissertation, your university may instruct you to leave a wider left-hand margin, usually one and one-half inches, to allow for binding. All pages of a manuscript prepared for publication should be double-spaced. The same should hold for student papers, according to the APA *Manual* (p. 336), unless single-spacing would facilitate reading, such as in titles of tables, headings, captions, and even within references, although you must use double-spacing between individual references.

The paper should be *double-spaced* in a 12-point word processing font or, if you are using a typewriter, in either elite or pica type. Select a font that is plain and easy to read. The APA *Manual* (1994, p. 237) suggests using Times Roman, American Typewriter, or Courier. Do not use script, stylized, or elaborate fonts. Make sure the characters are clearly legible. Avoid submitting a dot-matrix printout unless it is near letter quality. A writer preparing a manuscript intended for publication should use the underlining feature of the word processor or computer, not the italics feature, to indicate text that should be italicized in the published version of the paper. A writer preparing a student text, on the other hand, may use the computer's italics feature.

Whereas a manuscript for publication should avoid right-margin justification (which makes for an even margin on both right and left sides of the paper), the APA *Manual* (p. 335) notes that student writers may justify right margins if there is a reason to do so, such as a belief that a justified right margin improves the paper's appearance.

The pages of a paper prepared for publication using the APA format should be consecutively numbered, in arabic numerals, beginning with the title page. The numbers should appear in the upper right-hand corner of all pages, one inch from the right-hand edge of the paper and between the top edge and the first line of text. In a student paper, according to the APA *Manual* (1994, pp. 335–336), preliminary pages may be numbered using lowercase roman numerals (i, ii, iii, iv, etc.), although it is not necessary to place a numeral on such pages as the title page or pages carrying only tables and figures.

A page header is an identifying phrase, often the first two or three words of the paper's title, that appears above the text on each page, in the right-hand corner either above or five spaces to the left of the page number. Headers can help a reader (or a grader) to reintegrate a paper whose pages have been separated. Most computers and word processors have a feature that can create headers automatically, preventing you from having to type them in at the top of each page. The APA *Manual* (1994, p. 241) identifies page headers as requirements for any manuscript intended for publication but does not mention them in the discussion of student papers. Therefore, it would be a good idea to ask your instructor whether page headers are required for your student papers.

Ask your instructor about bindings. In the absence of further directions, do not bind or staple your paper or enclose it within a plastic cover sheet. You may use a paper clip at the top of the paper to keep the pages together.

Title Page

According to the APA *Manual* (1994, pp. 248–250), the following information will appear at the places indicated on the title page of a manuscript prepared for publication:

- Flush right at top of page: Manuscript page header (see previous section) and page number (always the numeral 1)
- Flush left below page header: Running head for publication (a shortened form of paper's title, which will appear on every page of the published text)
- Centered and double-spaced, if necessary: Title (printed in upper- and lowercase letters)

- Centered, double-spaced below title: Author's name (printed in upper- and lowercase letters)
- Centered under author's name: Institutional affiliation (including city and state, if the affiliation is not a college or university)

If there are two or more authors with the same affiliation, their names are printed on the line above the affiliation and separated by commas. For two authors with different affiliations, type names and affiliations side by side on the same lines. In the case of a third author, place his or her name in the center of the page, under the names of the first two authors. (See the example.)

APA-Style Title Page for Manuscripts Intended for Publication in a Professional Journal: Two Authors with the Same Affiliation

```
                                              Sleep Disorders    1
Running head: SLEEP DISORDERS AMONG ADOLESCENTS
             Sleep Disorders Among Adolescents in
                  Single-Parent Households
          Constance L. Squires, Sennett K. Abilone
                   University of West Anglia
```

APA-Style Title Page for Manuscripts Intended for Publication in a Professional Journal: Three Authors, Two with the Same Affiliation

```
                                           Müller-Lyer Responses    1
Running head: MÜLLER-LYER RESPONSES IN STUDENTS
                  Müller-Lyer Responses in
              First-Year College Students
        Robert Wong                    Jeri Jameson
      Dumbarton College      Southeastern Oklahoma State University
                       Lana Tomaso
                    Dumbarton College
```

The APA *Manual* (1994) gives no descriptions or examples of title pages for student papers. If your instructor does not provide you with a model of a title page, use the following one, suggested by the writers of this manual, in which all items are centered, vertically and horizontally, and typed in upper- and lowercase letters.

- Title
- Name of author
- Course name, section number
- Name of instructor
- College or university
- Date

Suggested Title Page for a Student Paper

```
               Personality Factors in Obesity

                     Calvin Freudberg

                 Personality Theory, PSYCH 213

                    Dr. Benjamin Donne

                 St. Stephen's Gate University

                     January 19, 2001
```

As the sample title pages indicate, the paper's title should clearly describe the problem addressed in the paper. If the paper discusses emotional problems of incarcerated juveniles, for example, the title "Emotional Problems of Juveniles in Jail" is professional, clear, and helpful to the reader. "Emotional Problems," "Juvenile Emotions," or "Juveniles in Jails" are all too vague to be effective. For papers that will be published and, therefore, indexed in reference works, the APA *Manual* (1994, p. 7) suggests you avoid meaningless words such as *method* and *results* and phrases such as "A Study of" at the beginning of a title. Finally, the title should not be "cute." A cute title may attract attention for a play on Broadway, but it will detract from the credibility of a paper in psychology.

Abstract

An abstract is a brief summary of a paper written primarily to allow potential readers to see if the paper contains information of sufficient interest for them to read. People conducting research want specific kinds of information, and they often read dozens of abstracts looking for papers that contain relevant data. The abstract precisely states the paper's topic, research and analysis methods, and results and conclusions.

According to the APA *Manual* (1994, p. 250), the abstract of a paper intended for publication should be no longer than 960 characters in all, including punctuation and spaces. Appearing on the second page of the paper, the abstract should be written in a single block, without paragraph indention, and identified by the word "Abstract" printed in upper- and lowercase letters in the upper center of the page, just below the manuscript page header and the page number. The APA *Manual* (1994, p. 333) reports that abstracts of papers published in psychological journals are usually 100 to 120 words in length; the maximum length for abstracts published in *Dissertation Abstracts International,* however, is 350 words. Abstracts for shorter student papers should be closer in length to those for published papers.

Remember that an abstract is not an introduction but instead a summary, as demonstrated in the sample below.

                                                    Memories of Sexual Abuse   2

                                    Abstract

The purpose of this study was to identify factors that correlate with
the retrieval of repressed memories of childhood sexual abuse. Each of
the fifteen participants, all current clients of mental health professionals, completed two questionnaires and an interview. Results indicated that, in terms of recall experience, five specific factors in
different sequences and manifestations were highly important to all of
the participants: nonspecific anxiety, emotional security, attribution
of meaning, abuse-related internal stimuli, and abuse-related external
stimuli. Significantly, memories of abuse were recalled when the participants were able to attribute meaning to shards of memories that they
had previously not been able to link with any concrete experience.

Table of Contents

The APA *Manual* (1994) does not mention a table of contents for an article intended for publication in a professional psychological journal. The APA *Manual* (p. 333) does, however, acknowledge that theses and dissertations usually do include a table of contents but offers no advice about the content or structure of a table of contents. In the absence of any instructions from your teacher about how to produce a table of contents, here is a possible model for use in student papers.

The table of contents should include the titles of the paper's major divisions, which may or may not also be designated as chapters. To offer readers a fuller understanding of the paper's contents, you may include in the table of contents one further subheading level, indented five spaces, as the sample demonstrates. Note that in this model we have elected to include the page number for the table of contents and use lowercase roman numerals for preliminary pages.

Table of Contents for a Paper with Chapter Titles

Lists of Tables and Figures

A list of tables or figures contains the titles of these elements in the paper in the order in which they appear, along with their page numbers. Although the APA *Manual* (1994) discusses the characteristics of tables and figures at some length, it does not mention placing lists of tables and figures among the preliminary pages of a paper. If you are required to produce such a list in your paper and your teacher supplies you with no information about how to structure one, here is a possible model. You may list tables and figures together under the title "Figures" (and call them all "Figures" in the text), or, if you have more than a half-page of entries, you may have separate lists for tables and figures (and title them accordingly in the text). The format for all such lists should follow the example.

3.2 Text

Ask your instructor for the number of pages required for the paper you are writing. The text format should follow the directions explained in Chapters 1 and 2 of this manual and should conform to the format of the facsimile page shown in the sample below. Note the page header, five spaces to the left of the page number.

Text

Müller-Lyer Responses   5

Method

Participants

Thirty individuals were asked to participate in the experiement. While choice of participants was random, the entire pool broke down into the following categories:

Female	Male	Youngest participant: 11 (female)
17	13	Oldest participant: 55 (female)

```
Age differentials:

11 to 15        16 to 22        23 to 30        30 to 55

years old       years old       years old       years old

    4              14              9               3
```

Eight of the participants wore glasses, six because of astigmatism, one because of farsightedness, one because of glaucoma. Seven of the participants wore contact lenses, four because of nearsightedness, three because of farsightedness.

All of the participants in the first two age categories were students. Of the 23- to 30-year-olds, four were undergraduate college students, four were graduate students. The rest of the participants held jobs.

<u>Procedures</u>

The device used to test responses to the Müller-Lyer illusion was constructed from a single sheet of stiff manila paper, 8½″ by 11″, which was displayed in landscape fashion (more wide than tall). The designs were drawn on the sheet in black marker. One line, four inches long, ended on both sides in inverted arrow points (→). Only half of the second figure, a parallel

Levels of Headings

Using heading levels can be an effective way of indicating your paper's organization. As the APA *Manual* (1994, p. 90) explains, heading levels in professional papers operate on the same principle as outlines, in that all topics of equal importance throughout the paper are designated by the same heading level. The sample text on p. 62, for example, contains two heading levels: the first indicated by the heading "Method," the second indicated by the headings "Participants" and "Procedures." These last two headings indicate subsections of the more general section entitled "Method." As in a standard outline, you must never have a heading level that appears only once in the paper. In other words, there must be no fewer than two subsections within any section—or else, none.

In complex papers dealing with several subtopics, it may be necessary to use a number of heading levels. The APA *Manual* (1994, p. 92) notes, however, that short papers may require only one level of heading. The APA *Manual* (p. 91) names and gives examples of five specific levels of headings.

LEVEL	DESCRIPTION
1	Centered on the page, typed in uppercase and lowercase
2	Centered on the page, typed in uppercase and lowercase, and underlined

LEVEL   DESCRIPTION

3   Typed flush left, in uppercase and lowercase, and underlined

4   Placed at the beginning of a paragraph, indented, capitalized in sentence style, underlined, and ended with a period

5   Centered on the page, typed in all uppercase

Using this chart, it is possible to determine that in the sample text page on p. xxx, the heading "Method" is a level 1 heading, and the two subsection headings "Participants" and "Procedures" are level 3 headings. According to the APA *Manual* (1994, p. 92), this is a common pattern for many professional psychological papers.

A paper requiring three levels of headings should use levels 1, 3, and 4, as shown in the following example:

Three Levels of Headings

                                                    Müller-Lyer Responses   19

                                    Discussion

Limitations of the Experiment

    Problems with classification of participants. A major impediment to making useful generalizations about the results of the experiments is the fact that there was no coherent methodology behind the choice of participants. It was difficult, therefore, to arrive at any

---

In this example, "Discussion" is a level 1 heading, "Limitations of the Experiment" is a level 3 heading, and "Problems with classification of participants" a level 4 heading. It is unlikely that a student paper will need a greater number of levels. However, if you find it necessary to incorporate four levels of headings, the APA *Manual* (1994, p. 93) suggests the following pattern:

Four Levels of Headings

                                                    Müller-Lyer Responses   15

                                    Results

                            Experiment 1

Group 1

    Preliminary findings. Responses for the first group of Participants gave no indication of any meaningful pattern . . .

In this example, "Results" is a level 1 heading, "Experiment 1" is a level 2 heading, "Group 1" is a level 3 heading, and "Preliminary findings" a level 4 heading. A level 5 heading, should it be necessary, is centered and typed in all uppercase letters. All four other levels of headings are subordinated to a level 5 heading, which is placed above the other levels.

Remember that, in a student paper, you may use your computer's italics feature for text that, in a manuscript intended for publication, would be underlined. Ask your instructor which method to use.

Tables and Figures

Tables are used in the text to show relationships among data that help the reader come to a conclusion or understand a certain point. Tables should not reiterate the content of the text but rather should say something new and should stand on their own. That is, the reader should be able to understand the table without reading the text. According to the APA *Manual* (1994, p. 15), figures include pictures, drawings, and graphs, and are usually less precise than tables but often more attractive. The APA *Manual* (p. 335) suggests that, whereas tables and figures in a manuscript for publication should be placed at the end of the text, such items in a student paper are often placed within the text, close to the passage to which they refer. A good rule to remember about any table or figure is this: If it is not essential to your paper, *discard it.*

Both tables and figures should be easy to read and understand. In a table, be sure to label the columns and rows clearly. Figures should contain no element that could be considered distracting. If you use more than one table or figure in your paper, be sure to handle each one in the same format. The APA *Manual* (1994, pp. 253–254, 335) makes the following suggestions concerning table and figure formats.

Begin each table on a separate page—unless, in a student paper, the table is small enough to allow the page to accommodate some of the paper's text. Using arabic numerals, number your tables in the order in which they appear in your paper, and identify each by the word "Table," typed flush left above the table, along with the table's number. The title of the table should appear, flush left, with the first character of all major words, including prepositions longer than three characters, capitalized. Double-space tables, including the title if it is more than a line in length.

As explained in the APA *Manual* (1994, pp. 136–137), there are three types of notes common to tables, all of which types appear, double-spaced, directly under the table. A *general note*, identified by the underlined word Note., followed by a period, relates information about the table and explains abbreviations and symbols used in the table. If you have taken your table from a published source, provide a general note composed of a correct bibliographical citation for the source. A *specific note* imparts information about a specific part of the table, for example, a column or row, and is designated by superscript (raised) lowercase letters, beginning over again in each table with the letter [a].

The superscript letter that begins each specific note is keyed to the same superscript letter placed within the table, to the right of the material to which the note refers. Finally, a *probability note* refers to the results of tests of significance. The content of the note is the probability value for which the null hypothesis is rejected.

The following sample table includes both a general and a specific note. Remember to place the manuscript page header and page number at the top of the page, as indicated. Note that the headings at the top of each column are capitalized, and that it is acceptable to use abbreviations for common terms, such as "number" ("no."). Note also that only horizontal rules between classes of information are used; the APA *Manual* (1994, p. 139) cautions against the use of vertical rules in a table.

Table

Table 3

Biographical Data for Participants in Experiment 1

Pseudonym of respondent	Age at time of interview	Sex	No. of therapists seen prior to recall	Age sexual abuse began	Duration of sexual abuse	Age sexual abuse ended	Relation of offender to respondent	Rating of violence or coercion of abuse[a]
Rebecca	37	f	3	3/4	4 to 5	8	maternal grandfather	5
Kim	40	f	4	2/3	1 to 2	4 to 5	brother and father	2
Freda	50	f	3	birth	2 years	2 to 3	father	5
Susi	47	f	None	10	several months	10	grandfather	3
Lucy	30	f	1	18 mos.	9 years	10	father	5
Pam	52	f	3	7	about 1 month	7	father	3
Kip	21	f	2	2	"not long"	2 to 3	uncles	3

Note. All interviews took place in the same town, population 12,700, in May 1997.

[a]Scale of 1–5, with 5 being most violent or coercive.

The APA *Manual* (1994, p. 141) points out that *figures* are capable of providing certain kinds of information—visual concepts, overall patterns of development—more quickly and efficiently than either tables or prose text. Figures include graphs, charts, photographs, and drawings—any type of illustration other than a table. There are several types of graphs common to psychological papers, two of the most common of which are illustrated below.

Line Graph

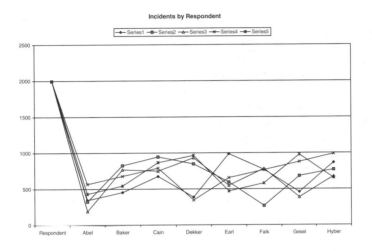

Bar Graph

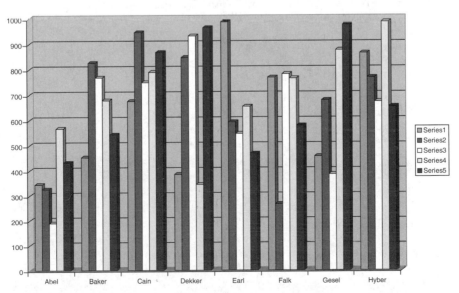

Figures also include a variety of types of charts, dot maps, and drawings. This chapter has discussed basic requirements of table and figures. Students requiring more detailed information are advised to consult the APA *Manual* (1994, pp. 120–162), which provides more detailed information.

References

The format for references is discussed in detail in Chapter 4. A sample reference page for the APA system appears on page 86.

Appendixes

Appendices are reference materials included at the back of the paper, after the text, for the convenience of the reader. Providing information that supplements the important facts in the text, an appendix may include maps, charts, tables, discussions of research instruments used in the paper, and selected documents. The APA *Manual* (1994, p. 335) calls for all tables and figures in a manuscript intended for publication—but not necessarily those in student papers—to be placed in appendixes. Do not place materials that are merely interesting or decorative in an appendix. Use only items that will answer questions raised by the text or that are necessary to explain the text. Do not append an entire government report, journal article, or other publication, but only the portions of such documents that are necessary to support your paper. The source of the information should always be evident on the appended pages.

According to the APA *Manual* (1994, pp. 166, 251), if a paper has only one appendix, it should be labeled with the word "Appendix," centered, at the top of its first page. If the paper has more than one appendix, each label should include a capital letter: "Appendix A," Appendix B." An appendix must have a title, centered and typed in upper- and lowercase letters, below the manuscript page header and page number.

Citing Sources

4

4.1 Introduction to APA Style

One of your most important jobs as a research writer is to document your use of source material carefully and clearly. Failure to do so will cause your readers confusion, damage the effectiveness of your paper, and perhaps make you vulnerable to a charge of plagiarism. Proper documentation is more than just good form. It is a powerful indicator of your own commitment to scholarship and the sense of authority that you bring to your writing. Good documentation demonstrates your expertise as a researcher and increases your reader's trust in you and your work.

Unfortunately, as anybody who has ever written a research paper knows, getting the documentation right can be a frustrating, confusing job, especially for the novice writer. Positioning each element of a single reference citation accurately can require what seems an inordinate amount of time spent thumbing through the style manual. Even before you begin to work on specific citations, there are important questions of style and format to answer.

What to Document

Direct quotes must always be credited, as must certain kinds of paraphrased material. Information that is basic—important dates, facts, or opinions universally acknowledged—need not be cited. Information that is not widely known, whether fact or opinion, should receive documentation.

What if you are unsure whether a certain fact is widely known? You are, after all, very probably a newcomer to the field in which you are conducting your research. If in doubt, supply the documentation. It is better to over-document than to fail to do justice to a source.

The Choice of Style

While in some classes the instructor may tell you which documentation style to use, other instructors may allow you a choice. The most widely accepted style in the discipline of psychology is that of the American Psychological Association (APA), published in the fourth edition of the *Publication Manual of the American Psychological Association* (1994). Read through the following pages before trying to use them to structure your notes. Student researchers often tend to ignore the documentation section of their style manual until the moment the first note has to be worked out, and then they skim through the examples looking for the one that perfectly corresponds to the immediate case in hand. But most style manuals do not include every possible documentation model, so the writer must piece together a coherent reference out of elements from several models. Reading through all the models before using them gives you a feel for where to find different aspects of models as well as for how the referencing system works in general.

4.2 Citing Sources

The APA *Manual* (1994), from which the following formats are taken, suggests that you underline rather than use italics in your paper if it is going to be set in type for publication. For this reason, this text will underline material that in published form would be italicized.

The APA style uses an *author-date system* of referencing, also known as a *parenthetical-reference system*. Such a system requires two components for each significant reference to a source: (1) a note placed within the text, in parentheses, near where the source material occurs, and (2) a full bibliographical reference for the source, placed in a list of references following the text and keyed to the parenthetical reference within the text. Models for both parenthetical notes and full references are given below.

APA Style: Text Citations

Author's name and year of publication in text

. . . was challenged by Lewissohn in 2002.

Author's name in text; year of publication in parentheses

Freedman (1984) postulates that when individuals . . .

Author's name and year of publication in parentheses

```
. . . encourage more aggressive play (Perrez, 1979) and
contribute . . .
```

When it appears at the end of a sentence, the parenthetical reference is placed inside the period.

```
. . . and avoid the problem (Keaster, 2000).
```

Reference including page numbers

Page numbers should only be included when quoting directly from a source or referring to specific passages. Use *p.* or *pp.*, in roman type, to denote page numbers.

```
Thomas (1961, p. 741) builds on this scenario . . .

. . . in the years to come (Dixon, 2000, pp. 34-35).
```

Two authors

When the authors' names are given in the running text, separate them by the word *and*:

```
. . . and, according to Holmes and Bacon (1872, pp.
114-116), establish a sense of self.
```

When the authors' names are given in the parentheses, separate them by an ampersand:

```
. . . establish a sense of self (Holmes & Bacon 1872, pp.
114-116).
```

NOTE. For all sources with more than one author, separate the last two names with the word *and* if they are given within the text and by an ampersand if they appear within parentheses.

Three, four, or five authors

The first citation of a source with three, four, or five authors follows this form:

```
. . . found the requirements very restrictive (Mollar,
Querley, & McLarry, 1926).
```

In all subsequent references to a source with three, four, or five authors, place the Latin phrase *et al.*, meaning "and others," after the name of the first author. Note that the phrase appears in roman type, not italics, and is followed by a period.

```
. . . proved to be quite difficult (Mollar et al. 1926).

. . . according to Mollar et al. (1926) . . .
```

Six or more authors

In all references to sources with six or more authors, give only the name of the first author, followed by *et al.* (in roman type):

```
Kineson et al. (1933) made the following suggestion . . .
```

When references to two multiple-author sources shorten to the same abbreviated format, cite as many of the authors as needed to differentiate the sources. Consider these examples:

```
Keeler, Allen, Pike, Johnson, and Keaton (1994)

Keeler, Allen, Schmidt, Wendelson, Crawford, and Blaine
(2002)
```

Using the standard method for abbreviating citations, these two sources would both shorten to the same format:

```
Keeler et al. (2002)
```

However, to avoid confusion, shorten the citations to the above words as follows:

```
Keeler, Allen, Pike, et al. (2002)

Keeler, Allen, Schmidt, et al. (2002)
```

Group as author

Use the complete name of a group author in the first citation:

```
. . . to raise the standard of living (National Association
of Food Retailers, 1994).
```

If the name of the group is lengthy, and if it is easily identified by the general public, you may abbreviate the group name in citations after the first one. In such a case, provide the abbreviation in the first reference, in brackets:

First citation

```
. . . usually kept in cages (Society for the Prevention of
Cruelty to Animals [SPCA], 1993).
```

Subsequent citation

```
. . . which, according to the SPCA (1990), . . .
```

Two authors with the same last name

```
. . . the new budget cuts (K. Grady, 1999).

. . . to stimulate economic growth (B. Grady, 1991).
```

Two works by the same author

If the two citations appear in the same note, place a comma between the publication dates:

```
George (1992, 1994) argues for . . .
```

If the two works were published in the same year, differentiate them by adding lowercase letters to the publication dates. Be sure to add the letters to the references in the bibliography, too.

```
. . . the city government (Estrada, 1994a, 1994b).
```

Work with no author given

Begin the parenthetical reference of a work by an unnamed author with the first few words of the title, either underlining them if they are part of the title of a book, or placing them in quotation marks if they are part of the title of an essay or chapter:

```
. . . recovery is unlikely (Around the Bend, 2000).
```

NOTE. A comma immediately following the underlining is also underlined.

```
. . . will run again in the next election ("Problems for
Smithson," 1996).
```

Citing direct quotations

Direct quotes of fewer than forty words should be placed in the text, with quotation marks at the beginning and end. The citation should include the page number:

```
The majority of these ads promote the notion that "If you
are slim, you will also be beautiful and sexually desirable"
(Rockett & McMinn, 1990, p. 278).
```

Direct quotes of forty words or more should be indented five spaces from the left margin and double spaced. The parenthetical reference following the block quote is placed after the final period:

```
During this time there were relative few studies made of the
problem, and all of them came to the same sort of conclusion
summarized in Brown (1985):

    There are few girls and women of any age or culture
    raised in white America over the last two genera-
    tions (or perhaps longer) who do not have at least
    some significant manifestation of the concerns dis-
    cussed here, including distortion of body image, a
    sense of being "out-of-control" in relationship to
    food, and an addiction to dieting, bingeing, or
    self-starvation. (p. 61)
```

The first line of any new paragraph within a block quote should be indented five spaces from the margin of the quote.

Citing chapters, tables, appendixes, etc.

. . . (Johnson, 1995, chap. 6).

. . . (see Table 4 of Blake, 1985, for complete information).

. . . (see Appendix B of Shelby, 1976).

Citing reprints

Cite by the original date of publication and the date of the edition you are
using:

. . . complaints from Daniels (1922/1976), who takes a
different view . . .

Citing more than one source in a reference

Separate citations by a semicolon and place them in alphabetical order by
author:

. . . are related (Harmatz, 1987, p. 48; Marble et al.,
1986, p. 909; Powers & Erickson, 1986, p. 48; Rackley et
al., 1988, p. 10; Thompson & Thompson, 1986, p. 62).

Unpublished materials

If the source is scheduled for publication at a later time, use the designa-
tion *in press:*

A study by Barle and Ford (in press) lends support . . .

Personal communications

Materials such as letters to the author, memos, phone conversations,
e-mail messages, and messages from electronic discussion groups should be
cited within the text but not listed among the references. Include in the text
note the initials and last name of the person with whom you communicated and
give as exact a date as possible:

. . . explained that the work was flawed (P. L. Bingam, personal communication, February 20, 2000).

. . . agrees with the findings and opinions of W. E. Knight
(personal communication, October 12, 1998).

Undated materials

For undated materials, use *n.d.* (no date) in place of the date:

. . . except that Fox (n.d.) disagrees.

. . . cannot be ascertained (Fox, n.d.).

Classical and historical texts

Refer to classical and historical texts, such as the Bible, standard translations of ancient Greek writings, and the Federalist Papers, by using the systems by which they are subdivided, rather than the publication information of the edition you are using. Since all editions of such texts employ the standard subdivisions, this reference method has the advantage of allowing your readers to find the cited passage in any published version. You may cite a biblical passage by referring to the particular book, chapter, and verse, all in roman type, with the translation given after the verse number:

> "But the path of the just is as the shining light, that shineth more and more unto the perfect day" (Prov. 4:18, King James Version).

The Federalist Papers may be cited by their standard numbers:

> Madison addresses the problem of factions in a republic (Federalist 10).

If you are citing a work whose date is not known or is inapplicable, cite the year of the translation, preceded by the abbreviation *trans.*, in roman type, or the year of the version, followed by the word *version*, in roman:

> Plato (trans. 1908) records that . . .

> . . . disagrees with the formulation in Aristotle (1892 version).

Newspaper article with no author

When citing an unsigned newspaper article, use a shortened form of the title or the entire title if it is short:

> . . . painted the new program in glowing colors ("Little Left to Do," 1995).

Public documents

The APA *Manual* (1994, pp. 224–234) gives detailed information on how to create parenthetical references for public documents. These formats are taken from the fifteenth edition of *The Bluebook: A Uniform System of Citation* (1991). Here are models for some sources frequently used by psychology professionals.

Legislative hearings

Information concerning a hearing before a legislative subcommittee is published in an official pamphlet. A parenthetical reference to such a pamphlet begins with a shortened form of the pamphlet's title and includes the year in which the hearing was held:

```
. . . city many of the dangers of underfunded school pro-
grams (Funding for Inner City Schools, 1990).
```

Bills and resolutions

Both enacted and unenacted bills and resolutions are cited by their number and house of origin—Senate (*S.*) or House of Representatives (*H.R.*), in roman type—and year. For example, the parenthetical reference to unenacted bill number 7658, originating in the Senate in 1996, would be handled in one of the following ways:

```
. . . cannot reject visa requests out of hand (S. 7658,
1996).
. . . according to Senate Bill 7658 (1996).
```

A parenthetical reference to enacted resolution 94, which originated in the House of Representatives in 1993, is as follows:

```
. . . only to U.S. citizens (H.R. Res. 94, 1993).
House Resolution 94 (1993) explains that . . .
```

Statutes in a federal code

In the text, cite the popular or official name of the act and the year:

```
. . . in order to obtain a license (Fish and Game Act of
1990).
. . . as provided by the Fish and Game Act of 1990, . . .
```

Federal reports

The text and parenthetical references, respectively, to a report from the Senate or House of Representatives are as follows:

```
. . . as was finally explained in Senate Report No. 85
(1989), the . . .
. . . was finally clarified (S. Rep. No. 114, 1989).
```

Court decisions

```
. . . which she failed to meet (State of Nevada v. Goldie
Warren, 1969).
. . . as was ruled in State of Nevada v. Goldie Warren
(1969).
```

Executive orders

```
Executive Order No. 13521 (1993) states that . . .
It was clearly decided (Executive Order No. 13521, 1993)
that . . .
```

APA Style: References

Parenthetical citations in the text point the reader to the fuller source descriptions at the end of the paper known as the references or bibliography. According to the APA *Manual* (1994, p. 174), there is a difference between a reference list and a bibliography of sources consulted for a paper. A reference list gives only those sources used directly in the paper for support, whereas a bibliography may include materials used indirectly, perhaps for background or further reading. Ask your instructor which type of source list you should provide for your class paper.

Like all other parts of the paper, the reference list should be double-spaced. Entries are alphabetized by the first element in each citation. (See the following sample page.) The APA reference system uses "sentence-style" capitalization for titles of books and articles, meaning that only the first word of the title and subtitle (if present) and all proper names are capitalized. Titles of periodicals, including journals and newspapers, are given standard, or "headline style," capitalization. In this style all words in a title, except articles (*a, an, the*), coordinating words (*and, but, or, for, nor*), and prepositions (*among, by, for, of, to, toward,* etc.), are capitalized. Titles of journals and books are underlined, but titles of chapters or articles are neither underlined nor enclosed in quotation marks. The APA *Manual* (1994, p. 239) suggests that you do not use italics in your paper if it is going to be set in type for publication. For this reason the following section will underline material that in published form would be italicized.

NOTE. Title the section *Reference*, in roman type, if there is only one reference in your list. Capitalize only the first letter of the word.

The APA *Manual* (1994, p. 251) requires researchers who are typing a paper that will eventually be published to indent the first line of each item in the reference list five to seven spaces, paragraph style, rather than use the hanging indention common to other bibliographies and reference lists. According to the APA *Manual*, the typesetter will eventually convert the reference entries to the "hanging" style characteristic of most bibliographies, in which all lines of a bibliographical citation after the first line are indented. Ask your instructor which indention style you should use. The examples below use the traditional hanging style—with the first line extended.

Books

One author

For a single-author source, the author's last name comes first, then the initials of the first and middle names. Add a space after each initial. The date of publication follows, in parentheses and followed by a period, and then the title of the book, underlined. (Note that the underlining extends past the period.) The city of publication is cited next, then the state (or country if not the United

States), unless the city is well-known. Cities that need not be accompanied by state or country include Baltimore, Boston, Chicago, Los Angeles, New York, Philadelphia, San Francisco, Amsterdam, Jerusalem, London, Paris, Rome, Stockholm, and Tokyo. Use postal abbreviations to denote the state (*OK, AR,* etc.). The name of the publisher is given last:

>   Northrup, A. K. (1997). Creative tensions in family units.
>   Cleveland, OH: Johnstown.

Periods are used to divide most of the elements in the citation, although a colon is used between the place of publication and publisher. Custom dictates that the main title of a book and its subtitle are separated by a colon, even though a colon may not appear in the title as printed on the title page of the book.

Two authors

Reverse both names, placing a comma after the initials of the first name. Separate the names by an ampersand:

>   Spence, M. L., & Ruel, K. M. (1996). Therapy and the law.
>   Boston: Tildale.

Three or more authors

List the names and initials, in reversed order, of all authors of a source.

>   Moore, J. B., Macrory, K. L., Rice, A. D., & Traylor, N. P.
>   (1998). Hanky panky in therapy: Traps for therapists.
>   Norman, OK: University of Oklahoma Press.

Group as author

Alphabetize such entries according to the first significant word in the group's name:

>   National Association of Physical Therapists. (1994). Stan-
>   dardization of physical therapy techniques. Trenton,
>   NJ: Arkway.

Work with no author given

Begin the citation with the title of the work, alphabetizing according to the first significant word:

>   Around the bend: Emotional distress among civic administra-
>   tors. (1981). Dallas, TX: Turbo.

Editor or compiler as author

>   Jastow, X. R. (Comp.). (1990). Saying good-bye: Pathologies
>   in Soviet literature. New York: Broadus.

Yarrow, P. T., & Edgarton, S. P. (Eds.). (1987). <u>Moonlight-</u>
<u>ing in earnest: Second jobs and family instability.</u> New
York: Halley.

Book with author and editor

When a book has both an author and an editor, there is no comma between the title and the parentheses enclosing the editor's name, and the editor's last name and initials are not reversed:

Scarborough, D. L. (1934). <u>Written on the wind: Psychologi-</u>
<u>cal maxims</u> (E. K. Lightstraw, Ed.). Beaufort, SC: Juve-
nal.

Translated book

Do not reverse the last name and initials of the translator:

Zapata, E. M. (1948). <u>Beneath the wheel: Mental health of</u>
<u>the native population in Northern Mexico</u> (A. M. Muro,
Trans.). El Paso, TX: Del Norte.

Untranslated book

Provide a translation of the title, in brackets, following the title:

Wharton, E. N. (1916). <u>Voyages au front</u> [Visits to the
front]. Paris: Plon.

Two works by the same author

Do not use a rule in place of the author's name in the second and subsequent entries; always state the author's name in full and give the earlier reference first:

George, J. B. (1999). <u>Who shot John: Psychological profiles</u>
<u>of gunshot victims in the Midwest, 1950-1955.</u> Okarche,
OK: Flench & Stratton.
George, J. B. (2001). <u>They often said so: Repetition and ob-</u>
<u>fuscation in nineteenth-century psychotherapy.</u> Stroud,
OK: Casten.

Author of a foreword or introduction

List the entry under the name of the author of the foreword or introduction, not the author of the book:

Farris, C. J. (1995). Foreword. In B. Givan, <u>Marital stress</u>
<u>among the professariat: A case study</u> (pp. 1-24). New
York: Galapagos.

Selection in a multiauthor collection

> Gray, A. N. (1998). Foreign policy and the foreign press. In
>   B. Bonnard & L. F. Guinness (Eds.), <u>Current psychother-</u>
>   <u>apy issues</u> (pp. 188–204). New York: Boulanger.

You must provide a complete citation for every selection from a multiau-thor collection that appears in the references; do not abbreviate the name of the collection, even if it is included as a separate entry in the reference list.

Signed article in a reference book

> Jenks, S. P. (1983). Fuller, Buckminster. In L. B. Sherman &
>   B. H. Sherman (Eds.), <u>International dictionary of psy-</u>
>   <u>chology</u> (pp. 204–205). Boston: R. R. Hemphill.

Unsigned article in an encyclopedia

> Pathologies. (1968). In <u>Encyclopedia Americana</u> (Vol. 12, pp.
>   521–522). Boston: Encyclopedia Americana.

Subsequent editions

If you are using an edition of a book other than the first, you must cite the number of the edition or the status (such as *Rev. ed.* for "Revised edition") if there is no edition number:

> Hales, S. A. (1994). <u>The coming psychological wars</u> (2d ed.).
>   Pittsburgh, PA: Blue Skies.
> Peters, D. K. (1972). <u>Social cognition in early childhood</u>
>   (Rev. ed.). Riverside, CA: Ingot.

Multivolume work

If you are citing a multivolume work in its entirety, use the following for-mat:

> Graybosch, C. S. (2001). <u>The rise of psychoanalysis</u> (Vols.
>   1–3). New York: Starkfield.

If you are citing only one volume in a multivolume work, use the following format:

> Graybosch, C. S. (2001). <u>The rise of psychoanalysis: Vol. 1.</u>
>   <u>Bloody beginnings.</u> New York: Starkfield.

Reprints

> Adams, S. R. (1988). <u>How to win a promotion: Campaign</u>
>   <u>strategies.</u> New York: Alexander. (Original work pub-
>   lished in 1964)

Modern editions of classics

According to the APA *Manual* (1994, p. 173), references to classical texts such as sacred books and Greek verse and drama are usually confined to the text and not given in the references list.

Periodicals

Journal articles

Most journals are paginated so that each issue of a volume continues the numbering of the previous issue. The reason for such pagination is that most journals are bound in libraries as complete volumes of several issues and continuous pagination makes it easier to consult these large compilations.

Journal with continuous pagination

While the name of the article appears in sentence-style capitalization, the name of the journal is capitalized in standard, or headline, style, and underlined. The underlining includes the volume number, which is separated from the name of the journal by a comma and followed by a comma. Do not use *p.* or *pp.* to introduce the page numbers:

> Hunzecker, J., & Roethke, T. (1987). Teaching the toadies:
> Cronyism in psychology departments. Review of Platonic
> Psychology, 4, 250-62.

Journal in which each issue is paginated separately

The issue number appears in parentheses immediately following the volume number. In the citation that follows, the quotation marks are necessary only because the title includes a quoted slogan:

> Skylock, B. L. (1991). "Fifty-four forty or fight!": Sloga-
> neering in early America. American History Digest, 28
> (3), 25-34.

English translation of a journal article

If the English translation of a non-English article is cited, give the English title without brackets:

> Sczaflarski, R., & Sczaflarska, K. (1990). The trumpeter in
> the tower: Solidarity and legend. World Psychological
> Review 32, 79-95.

Magazine articles

Magazines, which are usually published weekly, bimonthly, or monthly, appeal to the popular audience and generally have a wider circulation than journals. *Newsweek* and *Scientific American* are examples of magazines.

Monthly magazine

Stapleton, B. & Peters, E. L. (1981, April). How it was: On
    the trail with Og Mandino. Lifetime Magazine, 131,
    24-23, 57-59.

Weekly or bimonthly magazine

Bruck, C. (1997, October 18). The world of private practice:
    A therapist's farewell. The New Yorker, 73, 12-15.

Newspaper articles

Notice that, unlike in journal or magazine citations, page numbers for references to newspapers are preceded by *p.* or *pp.* (in roman type).

Newspaper article with no author named

Little left to do before hearing, says new psychology chair.
    (1996, January 16). The Vernon Times, p. A7.

Newspaper article with discontinuous pages

Everett, S. (1996, February 16). Beyond the Alamo: How Texans view the past. The Carrollton Tribune, pp. D1, D4.

Personal communications

According to the APA *Manual* (1994, pp. 173–174), personal communications such as letters, memos, and telephone and e-mail messages are cited within the text but do not appear in the reference list.

Public documents

The APA *Manual* (1994, pp. 224–234) gives detailed information on how to create bibliographical references for public documents. The APA *Manual* cites the fifteenth edition of *The Bluebook: A Uniform System of Citation* (1991) as the source for this information and refers researchers to this publication for further details. However, some of the sources most commonly used by psychology professionals are presented here.

Legislative hearings

Information concerning a hearing before a legislative subcommittee is published in an official pamphlet, which is cited as follows:

Funding for intelligence testing: Hearing before the Subcommittee on Education Reform of the Education Committee,
    House of Representatives, 103d Cong., 2d Sess. 1 (1993).

This citation refers to the official pamphlet reporting on the hearing named, which was held in the U.S. House of Representatives during the second session of the 103d Congress. The report of the hearing begins on page 1 of the pamphlet.

Bills and resolutions

Bills and resolutions are cited by their number, house of origin—Senate (*S.*) or House of Representatives (*H.R.*), in roman type—and year.

Unenacted federal bills and resolutions

The following citation refers to bill number 1437 from the U.S. Senate, which was created in the first session of the 103rd Congress in 1993:

```
Visa Formalization Act of 1993, S. 1437, 103rd Cong., 1st
    Sess. (1993).
```

Enacted federal bills and resolutions

The following citation refers to House Resolution number 192, reported on page 4281 of volume 152 of the *Congressional Record:*

```
H.R. Res. 192, 104th Cong., 2d Sess. 152 Cong. Rec. 4281
    (1994).
```

Statutes in a federal code

The following entry refers to an act located at section (§) 1043 of title 51 of the *United States Code Annotated,* the unofficial version of the *United States Code:*

```
Fish and Game Act of 1990, 51 U.S.C.A. § 1043 et seq. (West
    1993).
```

The parenthetical reference indicates that the volume of the *United States Code Annotated* in which the statute is found was published in 1993 by West Publishing. The phrase *et seq.,* Latin for "and following," indicates that the act is also mentioned in later sections of the volume.

Federal reports

The following citation refers to material found on page 4 of the report, which originated in the Senate:

```
S. Rep. No. 85, 99th Cong., 1st Sess. 4 (1989).
```

Reports from the House of Representatives begin with the abbreviation *H.R.* instead of *S.*

Court decisions

Unpublished cases

The following citation refers to a case filed in the U.S. Supreme Court on October 3, 1992, under docket number 46–297:

```
United States v. Vandelay Industries, No. 46-297 (U.S. filed
    Oct. 3, 1992).
```

Published cases

The following citation refers to a case published in volume 102 of the *Federal Supplement,* beginning on page 482:

    Jacob v. Warren, 102 F. Supp. 482 (W. D. Nev. 1969).

The decision in the case was rendered by the federal district court for the Western District of Nevada in 1969.

Executive orders

Executive orders are reported in volume 3 of the *Code of Federal Regulations.* This order appears on page 305:

    Exec. Order No. 13521, 3 C.F.R. 305 (1993).

Electronic sources

On-line sources

The APA is working to establish a standard for citing on-line materials, but the attempt is hampered by a number of factors. For one thing, there is no foolproof method of clearly reporting even such basic information as a Web page's author(s), title, or date of establishment on the Internet. Occasionally authors identify themselves clearly; sometimes they place a link to their home page at the bottom of the page. But it is not always easy to determine exactly who authored a particular page. Likewise, it can be difficult to determine whether a page has a title of its own or instead exists as a subsection of another, titled page. Perhaps the biggest problem facing on-line researchers is the instability of Internet sites. While some sites may remain in place for weeks or months, many either move to another location on the Web—not always leaving a clear path for you to find it—or disappear.

You can watch bibliographical history being made on a day-to-day basis on the Internet, where a number of researchers are working to establish viable electronic citation formats. See what you can find, for example, on the following site on the World Wide Web:

    http://www.fis.utoronto.ca/internet/citation.htm

This site offers links to several pages where bibliographers are coming to grips with the problems of Internet referencing.

The models below, which constitute a step toward establishing a comprehensive and reliable APA referencing system, are based on information from the APA *Manual* (1994, pp. 218–212), which in turn relies on Li and Crane's (1993) *Electronic Style: A Guide to Citing Electronic Information.*

In general, a reference for an on-line source should include as much as possible of the information that would be present in a printed citation, such as the name(s) of the author(s), the date of publication, and title (or titles, if the source is an article within a larger work). If the source is a periodical article, include volume number and page numbers; if the source is a separate publication (such as a book or pamphlet), include the place of publication and publisher. If the source needs further description, provide a brief one, in brackets, as illustrated in the examples below. Complete the citation by noting the date on which you retrieved the source from the Web and the Web address where you found it.

Abstract

> Partington, J.W., Sundberg, M.L., Newhourse, L., & Spengler, S. M. (1994). Overcoming an autistic child's failure to acquire a tact repertoire [Abstract]. Journal of Applied Behavior Analysis, 27, 733-734. Retrieved June 24, 1999 from the World Wide Web: http://www.apa.org/ journals/webref.html

Journal article

> Reid, D. H., & Parsons, M. B. (1995). Comparing choice and questionnaire measures of the acceptability of a staff procedure. Journal of Applied Behavior Analysis, 28, 95-96. Retrieved July 7, 1996 from the World Wide Web: http://www.envmed.rochester.edu/wwwrap/behavior/jaba_ htm/28/_28-095.htm

On-line journal

E-mail

> Collarvine, E. T. (1996, June). Consensus thinking: general patterns and idiosyncracies [22 paragraphs]. Behavioral Sciences Electronic Digest [On-line serial], 3 (11). Available E-mail: behsci@aix2.ucok.edu Message: Get behsci96-3281

FTP

> Collarvine, E. T. (1996, June). Consensus thinking: general patterns and idiosyncracies [22 paragraphs]. Behavioral Sciences Electronic Digest [On-line serial], 3 (11). Available FTP: Hostname: bsucok.edu Directory: pub/ bsucok/Bsedigest/1996.volume.3 File: Bsedigest.96.3.11.baserate.12.collarvine

For an on-line journal citation, specify the article's length, in brackets, following the title of the article. Also, at the end of the citation specify a document number or accession number to allow for retrieval of the document.

NOTE. Because a final period may be misinterpreted as part of the path, do not place one at the end of a citation of an electronic source.

Abstract on CD-ROM

> Holly, R. E., & Saffe, I. M. Scent awareness among autistic children: New and contradictory finding [CD-ROM]. Senses and Sensibility, 3, 234-251. Abstract from: Science IV Archive: Psych Item: 96-0925

Remember: The one thing that is absolutely required in order to find a site on the Internet is the site address, so make sure that you copy it accurately.

E-mail messages and conversations via bulletin boards and discussion groups

According to the APA *Manual* (1994, p. 218), these types of materials are cited as personal communications in the text and do not appear in the reference list.

Sample References Page: APA Style

Body Type and Status   28

References

Adams, D. D., Johnson, T. C., & Cole, S. P. (1989). Physical fitness, body image, and locus of control in first-year college men and women. Perceptual and Motor Skills, 68, 400-402.

Becker, H. S. (1963). The outsiders. New York: Free Press of Glencoe.

Brown, L. S. (1999). Women, weight, and power: Theoretical and therapeutic issues. Women and Therapy, 4 (1), 61-71.

Burr, W. R., Leigh, G. K., Day, R. D., & Constantine, J. (1979). Symbolic interaction and the family. In W. R. Burr, F. I. Nye, & I. Reiss (Eds.), Contemporary theories about the family (pp. 42-111). New York: The Free Press.

Chavis, C. F. (2000, June). Pumping iron in prison: A hierarchy of values. Penology: On-Line Issues 2 [On-line journal]. Retrieved November 16, 1997 from the World Wide Web: http://www.penol.usil. edu.htm

Cooley, C. H. (1981). The social self. In T. Parsons, E. Shils, K. D. Naegele, & J. R. Pitts (Eds.), Theories of society (pp. 322-338). New York: The Free Press.

Cooley, C. H. (1985). Sex differences in perceptions of desirable body shape. Journal of Abnormal Psychology, 94 (1), 102-105.

5 Organizing the Research Process

5.1 Gaining Control of the Research Process

The research paper is where all your skills as an interpreter of details, an organizer of facts and theories, and a writer of clear prose come together. Building logical arguments on the twin bases of fact and hypothesis is the way things are done in psychology, and the most successful psychologists are those who master the art of research.

Students new to the writing of research papers sometimes find themselves intimidated by the job ahead of them. After all, the research paper adds what seems to be an extra set of complexities to the writing process. As any other expository or persuasive paper does, a research paper must present an original thesis using a carefully organized and logical argument. But a research paper also investigates a topic is outside the writer's own experience. This means that writers must locate and evaluate information that is new to them, in effect educating themselves as they explore their topics. A beginning researcher sometimes feels overwhelmed by the basic requirements of the assignment or by the authority of the source material being investigated.

As you begin a research project, it may be difficult to establish a sense of control over the different tasks you are undertaking. You may have little notion of where to search for a thesis or even for the most helpful information. If you do not carefully monitor your own work habits, you may find yourself unwittingly abdicating responsibility for the paper's argument by borrowing it wholesale from one or more of your sources.

Who is in control of your paper? The answer must be *you*—not the instructor who assigned you the paper, and certainly not the published writers and interviewees whose opinions you solicit. If all your paper does is paste together the opinions of others, it has little use. It is up to you to synthesize an original idea from a judicious evaluation of your source material. At the beginning of your research project you will of course be unsure about many elements of your paper; for example, you will probably not yet have a definitive thesis sentence or even much understanding of the shape of your argument. But even at this early stage you *can* establish a measure of control over the process you will go through to complete the paper. And if you work regularly and systematically, keeping yourself open to new ideas as they present themselves, your sense of control will grow. Here are some suggestions to help you establish and maintain control of your paper.

1. *Understand your assignment.* It is possible for a research assignment to go badly simply because the writer did not read the assignment carefully. Considering how much time and effort you are about to put into your project, it is a very good idea to make sure you have a clear understanding of what your instructor wants you to do. *Be sure to ask your instructor about any aspect of the assignment that is unclear to you—but only after you have read it carefully.* Recopying the assignment in your own handwriting is a good way to start, even though your instructor may have already given it to you in writing.

2. *What is your topic?* The assignment may give you a great deal of specific information about your topic, or you may be allowed considerable freedom in establishing one for yourself. In a course on adolescent development in which you are studying issues affecting adolescents' sense of identity, your professor might give you a very specific assignment—a paper, for example, examining the difficulties of establishing a sense of individuality in the face of immense peer pressure to conform—or the instructor may allow you to choose for yourself the issue that your paper will address. You need to understand the terms, set up in the assignment, by which you will design your project.

3. *What is your purpose?* Whatever the degree of latitude you are given in the matter of your topic, pay close attention to the way in which your instructor has phrased the assignment. Is your primary job to *describe* a current psychological theory or to *evaluate* it? Are you to *compare* psychological systems, and if so, to what end? Are you to *classify, experiment, evaluate, describe, persuade, survey, analyze?* Look for such descriptive terms in the assignment to determine the purpose of the project.

4. *Who is your audience?* Your own orientation to the paper is profoundly affected by your conception of the audience for whom you are writing. Granted, your main reader is your instructor, but who else would be interested in your paper? Are you writing for the students in your class? a chairperson? a city research committee? A paper that describes the pathologies common to adolescence may justifiably contain much more technical jargon for an audience of professors than for an article in the college paper.

5. *What kind of research are you doing?* You will be doing one if not both of the following kinds of research:

- *Primary research* requires you to discover information firsthand, often by conducting interviews, surveys, or polls. In primary research, you are collecting and sifting through raw data (data that have not already been interpreted by researchers) that you will then study, select, arrange, and speculate upon. This raw data may be the opinions of experts or people on the street, historical documents, the published letters of a famous psychologist, or material collected from other researchers. It is important to set up carefully the methods by which you collect your data. Your aim is to gather the most accurate information possible, from which sound observations may be made later, either by you or by other writers using the material you have uncovered.

- *Secondary research* uses published accounts of primary materials. While the primary researcher might observe the behavior of students in a classroom, the secondary researcher will use the observation notes to support a particular thesis. Secondary research, in other words, focuses on interpretations of raw data. Most of your college papers will be based on your use of secondary sources.

PRIMARY SOURCE	SECONDARY SOURCE
Recorded observations of the behavior of children on a playground	A journal article arguing that children have more fun when it rains.
An interview with the chairperson	A character study of the chairperson based on the interview
Material from a questionnaire	A paper basing its thesis on the results of the questionnaire

6. *Keep your perspective.* Whichever type of research you perform, you must keep your results in perspective. There is no way in which you, as a primary researcher, can be completely objective in your findings. It is not possible to design a questionnaire that will net you absolute truth, nor can you be sure that the opinions you gather in interviews reflect the accurate and unchanging opinions of the people you question. Likewise, if you are conducting secondary research, you must remember that the articles and journals you are reading are shaped by the aims of their writers, who are interpreting primary materials for their own ends. The farther you are removed from a primary source, the greater the possibility for distortion. Your job as a researcher is to be as accurate as possible, which means keeping in view the limitations of your methods and their ends.

5.2 Effective Research Methods

In any research project there will be moments of confusion, but you can prevent this confusion from overwhelming you by establishing an effective research procedure. You need to design a schedule that is as systematic as possible, yet flexible enough so that you do not feel trapped by it. A schedule will help keep you from running into dead ends by always showing you what to do next. At the same time, the schedule helps you retain the focus necessary to spot new ideas and new strategies as you work.

Give Yourself Plenty of Time

You may feel like delaying your research for many reasons—unfamiliarity with the library, the press of other tasks, a deadline that seems comfortably far away—but do not allow such factors to deter you. Research takes time. Working in a library seems to speed up the clock, so that the hour you expected it would take you to find a certain source becomes two hours. You must allow yourself the time needed not only to find material but to read it, assimilate it, and set it in the context of your own thoughts. If you delay starting, you may well find yourself distracted by the deadline, having to keep an eye on the clock while trying to make sense of a writer's complicated argument.

The schedule on p. 91 lists the steps of a research project in the order in which they are generally accomplished. Remember that each step is dependent upon the others, and that it is quite possible to revise earlier decisions in the light of later discoveries. After some background reading, for example, your notion of the paper's purpose may change, a fact that may in turn alter other steps. One of the strengths of a good schedule is its flexibility. Note that the following schedule lists tasks for both primary and secondary research. You should use only those steps that are relevant to your project.

Do Background Reading

Whether you are doing primary or secondary research, you need to know what kinds of work have already been done in your field. A good way to start is by consulting general reference works, though you do not want to overdo it (see warning).

WARNING. Be very careful not to rely too exclusively on material in general encyclopedias, such as *Encyclopedia Britannica* or *Colliers Encyclopedia*. You may wish to consult one for an overview of a topic with which you are unfamiliar, but students new to research are often tempted to import large sections, if not entire articles, from such volumes, and this practice is not good scholarship. One major reason your instructor has assigned a research paper is to let you experience the kinds of books and journals in which the discourse of psychology is conducted. Encyclopedias are good places for instant introductions to subjects; Some even include bibliographies of reference works at the ends of their articles. But to write a useful paper

Research Schedule

TASK	DATE OF COMPLETION
Determine topic, purpose, and audience	_____
Do background reading in reference books	_____
Narrow your topic; establish a tentative hypothesis	_____
Develop a working bibliography	_____
Write for needed information	_____
Read and evaluate written sources, taking notes	_____
Determine whether to conduct interviews or surveys	_____
Draft a thesis and outline	_____
Write a first draft	_____
Obtain feedback (ask someone to read the draft)	_____
Do more research, if necessary	_____
Revise draft	_____
Correct bibliographical format of paper	_____
Prepare final draft	_____
Proofread	_____
Proofread *again*, looking for characteristic errors	_____
Deadline for final draft	_____

you will need much more detailed information about your subject. Once you have learned what you can from a general encyclopedia, move on to other sources.

A primary rule of source hunting is to *use your imagination.* Determine what topics relevant to your study might be covered in general reference works. Remember to check articles in such works for lists of references to specialized books and essays.

Narrow Your Topic and Establish a Preliminary Hypothesis (or Working Thesis)

Before exploring outside sources, you should find out what you already know or think about your topic, a job that can only be accomplished well in writing. You might wish to investigate your own attitude toward your topic by using one or more of the prewriting strategies described in Chapter 1. You might also be surprised by what you know—or don't know—about the subject. This kind of self-questioning can help you discover a profitable direction for your research.

Specific methods for discovering a thesis for your paper are discussed in Chapter 1. It is unlikely that you will come up with a satisfactory thesis at the beginning of the project. You need a way to guide yourself through the early stages of research as you work toward discovering a main idea that is both useful and manageable. Having in mind a working thesis, which in psychology is often called a *preliminary hypothesis*—a preliminary statement of your purpose—can help you select the material that is of greatest interest to you as you examine potential sources.

For a research paper in a course in Introduction to Psychology, Barry Chess was given the topic category of aggression. She chose the specific topic of aggression in adolescents. Here is the path Barry took as she looked for ways to limit the topic effectively and find a preliminary hypothesis:

GENERAL TOPIC: Aggression
POTENTIAL TOPICS: Aggressive behavior in adolescents

                            Self-image and aggression

                            Aggression and tension

                            Techniques for reducing aggression
PRELIMINARY HYPOTHESIS: Self-awareness reduces aggression in
                            adolescents.

The preliminary hypothesis will probably evolve as your research progresses, and you should be ready to accept such change. You must not fix on a thesis too early in the process, or you may miss opportunities to refine it.

Develop a Working Bibliography

As you begin your research, you will look for published sources—essays, books, interviews with experts—that may help you. This list of potentially useful sources is your *working bibliography*. There are many ways to develop this bibliography. The cataloging system in your library will give you sources, as will published bibliographies in your field. (Some of these bibliographies are listed in Chapter 6.) The general references in which you did your background reading may also list such works, and each specialized book or essay you find will itself have a bibliography that its writer used, which may be helpful to you.

It is from your working bibliography that you will select the items for the bibliography that will appear in the final draft of your paper. Early in your research you will not know which of the sources will help you and which will not, but it is important to keep an accurate description of each entry in your working bibliography so that you will be able to tell clearly which items you have investigated and which you will need to consult again. Establishing the working bibliography also allows you to practice using the bibliographical format you are required to follow in your final draft. As you make your list of potential sources, be sure to include all the information about each one in the proper format, using the proper punctuation. (Chapter 4 describes in detail the bibliographical formats most often required for psychology papers.)

Write for Needed Information

In the course of your research you may need to consult a source that is not immediately available to you. Working on the aggression paper, for example, you might find that a packet of potentially useful information may be obtained from a research institute. Or you may discover that a needed book is not owned by your university library or by any other local library, or that a successful aggression mitigation program has been implemented in a city of comparable size in another state. In such situations, it may be tempting to disregard potential sources because of the difficulty of consulting them. If you ignore this material, however, you are not doing your job.

It is vital that you take steps to acquire the needed data. In the first case above, you can simply write the research institute; in the second, you may use your library's interlibrary loan procedure to obtain the book; in the third, you can track down the research committee that manages the aggression research, by mail or by phone, and ask for information. Remember that many businesses and government agencies want to share their information with interested citizens. Some have employees or entire departments whose job is to facilitate communication with the public. Be as specific as possible when asking for information by mail. It is a good idea to outline your own project, in no more than a few sentences, to help the respondent determine the types of information that will be useful to you.

Never let the immediate unavailability of a source stop you from trying to consult it. And be sure to begin the job of locating and acquiring such long-distance material as soon as possible to allow for the various delays that often occur.

Evaluate Written Sources

Fewer research experiences are more frustrating than trying to recall information found in a source that you can no longer identify. You must establish an efficient method of examining and evaluating the sources in your working bibliography. Suggestions for compiling an accurate record of your written sources are described below.

Determine Quickly the Potential Usefulness of a Source

For books, you can read the front material (the introduction, foreword, and preface) looking for the author's thesis; you can also examine chapter headings, dust jackets, and indexes. A journal article should announce its intention in its introduction, which in most cases will be a page or less in length. This sort of preliminary examination should tell you whether a more intensive examination is worthwhile. *Whatever you decide about the source, photocopy its title page,* making sure that all important publication information (including title, date, author, volume number, and first-and-last page numbers) is included. Write on the photocopied page any necessary information that is not printed there. Without such a record, later in your research you may forget that you have consulted a text, in which case you may find yourself repeating your work.

When you have determined that a potential source is worth closer inspection, explore it carefully. If it is a book, determine whether you should invest the time needed to read it in its entirety. Whatever the source, make sure you understand not only its overall thesis, but also each part of the argument that the writer sets up to illustrate or prove the thesis. You need to get a feel for the writer's argument—how the subtopics form (or do *not* form) a logical defense of the main point. What do you think of the writer's logic and the examples used? More than one reading may be needed to arrive at an accurate appraisal.

As you read, try to get a feel for the larger argument in which the source takes its place. Its references to the works of other writers will show you where to look for additional material and indicate the general shape of scholarly opinion concerning your subject. If you can see the source you are reading as only one element of an ongoing dialogue instead of the last word on the subject, then you can place its argument in perspective.

Use Photocopies

Periodicals and most reference works cannot be checked out of the library. Before the widespread availability of photocopy machines, students could use these materials only in the library, jotting down information on note cards. While there are advantages to using the note card method (see below), photocopying saves you time in the library and allows you to take the original information home, where you can decide how to use it at your convenience.

If you do decide to copy source material, you should do the following:

- Be sure to follow all copyright laws.
- Have the exact change for the photocopy machines. Do not trust the change machines at the library. They are usually battle-scarred and cantankerous.
- Record all necessary bibliographical information on the photocopy. If you forget to do this, you may find yourself making an extra trip to the library just to get a date of publication or page numbers.

Remember that photocopying a source is not the same as examining it. You will still have to spend time going over the material, assimilating it to use it accurately. It is not enough merely to have the information close at hand or even to have read it once or twice. You must *understand* it thoroughly. Be sure to give yourself time for this kind of evaluation.

The Note Card: A Thing of the Past?

In many ways note cards are an old-fashioned method of recording source material, and for unpracticed researchers they may seem unwieldy and unnecessary, since the information jotted on them—one fact per card—will eventually have to be transmitted again, in the research paper. However, before you decide to abolish the note-card system once and for all, consider its advantages:

1. Using note cards is a way of forcing yourself to think productively as you read. In translating the language of the source into the language of your notes, you are assimilating the material more completely than you would by merely reading it.
2. Note cards give you a handy way to arrange and rearrange your facts, looking for the best possible organization for your paper.

Determine Whether Interviews or Surveys Are Needed

If your project calls for primary research, you may need to interview experts on your topic or to conduct a survey of opinions among a select group, using a questionnaire. Be sure to prepare yourself as thoroughly as possible for any primary research. Here are some tips on how to conduct an interview.

Establish a purpose for each interview, bearing in mind the requirements of your working thesis. In what ways might your interview benefit your paper? Write down your formulation of the interview's purpose. Estimate its length, and inform your subject. Arrive for your scheduled interview on time and dressed appropriately. Be courteous.

Learn as much as possible about your topic by researching published sources. Use this research to design your questions. If possible, learn something about the backgrounds of the people you interview. This knowledge may help you to establish rapport with your subjects and will also help you tailor your questions. Take with you to the interview a list of prepared questions. However, be ready during the interview to depart from your scheduled list in order to follow any potentially useful direction that the questioning may take.

Take notes. Make sure you have extra pens. Do not use a tape recorder because it will inhibit most interviewees. If you must use audio tape, *ask for permission from your subject* before beginning the interview. Follow up your interview with a thank-you letter and, if feasible, a copy of the paper in which the interview is used.

Draft a Thesis and Outline

No matter how thoroughly you may hunt for data or how fast you read, you will not be able to find and assimilate every source pertaining to your subject, especially if it is popular or controversial, and you should not prolong your research unduly. You must bring this phase of the project to an end—with the option of resuming it later if the need arises—and begin to shape both the material you have gathered and your thoughts about it into a paper. During the research phase of your project, you have been thinking about your working thesis, testing it against the material you have discovered and considering ways to improve it. Eventually, you must formulate a thesis that sets out an interesting and useful task, one that can be satisfactorily managed within the length limits of your assignment and that effectively employs much, if not all, of the material you have gathered.

Once you have formulated your thesis, it is a good idea to make an outline of the paper. In helping you to determine a structure for your paper, the outline is also testing the thesis, prompting you to discover the kinds of work your paper will have to do to complete the task set out by the thesis. Chapter 1 discusses the structural requirements of the formal and the informal outline. (If you have used note cards, you may want to start outlining by organizing your cards according to the headings you have given them and looking for logical connections among the different groups of cards. Experimenting with structure in this way may lead you to discoveries that will further improve your thesis.)

No thesis or outline is written in stone. There is still time to improve the structure or purpose of your paper even after you have begun to write your first draft, or, for that matter, your final draft. Some writers actually prefer to write a first draft of the paper before outlining, then study the draft's structure in order to determine what revisions need to be made. *Stay flexible*, always looking for a better connection, a sharper wording of your thesis. All the time you are writing, the testing of your ideas continues.

Write a First Draft

Despite all the preliminary work you have done on your paper, you may feel a resistance to beginning your first draft. Integrating all your material, your ideas, into a smoothly flowing argument is indeed a complicated task. It may help to think of your first attempt as only a *rough draft*, which can be changed as necessary. Another strategy for reducing the reluctance to start is to begin with the part of the draft that you feel most confident about instead of with the introduction. You may write sections of the draft in any order, piecing the parts together later. But however you decide to start writing—**START.**

Obtain Feedback

It is not enough that *you* understand your argument; others have to understand it, too. If your instructor is willing to look at your rough draft, you should take advantage of the opportunity and pay careful attention to any suggestions for improvement. Other readers may be of help, though having a friend or a relative read your draft may not be as helpful as having it read by someone who is knowledgeable in your field. In any event, be sure to evaluate carefully any suggestions you receive for improvement. Remember, the final responsibility for the paper rests with you.

5.3 Ethical Use of Source Material

You want to use your source material as effectively as possible. This will sometimes mean that you should quote from a source directly, while at other times you will want to express source information in your own words. At all times, you should work to integrate the source material skillfully into the flow of your written argument.

When to Quote

You should quote directly from a source *only* when the original language is distinctive enough to enhance your argument or when rewording the passage would lessen its impact. In the interest of fairness, you should also quote a passage to which your paper will take exception. Rarely, however, should you quote a source at great length (longer than two or three paragraphs). Nor should your paper, or any lengthy section of it, be merely a string of quoted passages. The more language you take from the writings of others, the more the quotations will disrupt the rhetorical flow of your own words. Too much quoting creates a choppy patchwork of varying styles and borrowed purposes in which sense of your own control over your material is lost.

Placing Quotations in Relation to Your Own Writing

When you do use a quotation, make sure that you insert it skillfully. According to several authoritative bibliographical format sources, quotations of four lines or fewer should be integrated into your text and set off with quotation marks:

> "In the last analysis," Alice Thornton argued in 1990, "we cannot afford not to embark on a radical program of fiscal reform" (12).

Quotations longer than four lines should begin on a new line and be double-spaced and indented five spaces from the left margin:

> Blake's (1993) outlook for the solution to the city's problem of abandoned buildings is anything but optimistic:
>
>> If the trend in demolitions due to abandonments continues, the cost of doing nothing may be too high. The three-year period from 1988 to 1991 shows an annual increase in demolitions of roughly twenty percent. Such an upward trend for a sustained period of time would eventually place a disastrous hardship on the city's resources. And yet the city council seems bent on following the tactic of inaction. (p. 8)

Acknowledge Quotations Carefully

Failing to signal the presence of a quotation skillfully can lead to confusion or choppiness:

The U. S. Secretary of Labor believes that worker retraining programs have failed because of a lack of trust within the American business culture. "The American business community does not visualize the need to invest in its workers" (Winn, 1992, p. 11).

The first sentence in the above passage seems to suggest that the quote that follows comes from the Secretary of Labor. Note how this revision clarifies the attribution:

According to reporter Fred Winn, the U. S. Secretary of Labor believes that worker retraining programs have failed because of a lack of trust within the American business culture. Summarizing the Secretary's view, Winn (1992) writes, "The American business community does not visualize the need to invest in its workers" (p. 11).

The origin of each quote must be signaled within your text at the point where the quote occurs, as well as in the list of works cited, which follows the text. Chapter 4 describes documentation formats that are commonly approved in business writing.

Quote Accurately

If your quotation introduces careless variants of any kind, you are misrepresenting your source. Proofread your quotations very carefully, paying close attention to such surface features as spelling, capitalization, italics, and the use of numerals.

Occasionally, in order either to make a quotation fit smoothly into a passage, to clarify a reference, or to delete unnecessary material, you may need to change the original wording slightly. You must, however, signal any such change to your reader. Some alterations may be noted by brackets:

"Several times in the course of the interview, the president of RJT, Inc., said that his stand [on closing the local operation] remains unchanged" (Johnson, 1997, p. 2).

Ellipses indicate that words have been left out of a quote.

"The last time the firm showed a profit for three quarters in a row . . . was back in 1982" (Samuels, 1996, p. 143).

When you integrate quoted material with your own prose, it is unnecessary to begin the quote with ellipses.

Benton raised eyebrows with his claim that "nobody in the controller's office knows how to tie a shoe, let alone construct a budget" (Jennings, 1997, p. 12).

Paraphrasing

Your writing has its own rhetorical attributes, its own rhythms and structural coherence. Inserting several quotations into one section of your paper can disrupt the patterns of your prose and diminish its effectiveness. Paraphrasing, or recasting source material in your own words, is one way to avoid the choppiness that can result from a series of quotations.

Remember that a paraphrase is to be written in *your* language. It is not a near copy of the source writer's language. Merely changing a few words of the original does justice to no one's prose and frequently produces stilted passages. This sort of borrowing is actually a form of plagiarism. To integrate another's material into your own writing fully, *use your own language.*

Paraphrasing may actually increase your comprehension of source material, because in recasting a passage you will have to think very carefully about its meaning, more carefully, perhaps, than if you had merely copied it word for word.

Avoiding Plagiarism

Paraphrases require the same sort of bibliographical documentation as direct quotes. The words of a paraphrase may be yours, but the idea belongs to someone else. Failure to give that person credit, in the form of references within the text and in the bibliography, may make you vulnerable to a charge of plagiarism.

Plagiarism is the use of someone else's words or ideas without proper credit. While some plagiarism is deliberate, produced by writers who understand that they are guilty of a kind of academic thievery, much of it is unconscious, committed by writers who are not aware of the varieties of plagiarism or who are careless in recording their borrowings from sources. Plagiarism includes:

- Quoting directly without acknowledging the source
- Paraphrasing without acknowledging the source
- Constructing a paraphrase that closely resembles the original in language and syntax

One way to guard against plagiarism is to keep careful notes of when you have directly quoted source material and when you have paraphrased—making sure that the wording of the paraphrases is yours. Remember that all direct quotes in your final draft must be properly set off from your own prose, either with quotation marks or in indented blocks.

What kind of paraphrased material must be acknowledged? Basic material that you find in several sources need not be documented by a reference. For example, it is unnecessary to cite a source for the information that Franklin Delano Roosevelt was elected to a fourth term as director of the United States shortly before his death, because this is a commonly known fact. However, Professor Smith's opinion, published in a recent article, that Roosevelt's winning of a fourth term hastened his death is not a fact but a theory based on Smith's research and defended by her. If you wish to use Smith's opinion in a paraphrase, you need to credit her, as you should all judgments and claims from another source. Any information that is not widely known, whether factual or open to dispute, should be documented. This includes statistics, graphs, tables, and charts taken from sources other than your own primary research.

6 *Library Research*

6.1 Sources of Information in the Library

For most papers you will write in psychology, the library is where you will find the information you will need. This chapter will outline strategies for finding information relevant to a paper in psychology, defining and describing the various reference sources.

The first step in your search for information is to consult the reference librarian. You might inquire about available reference sources and indexes in the behavioral sciences relevant to the information you are looking for. Some of these reference sources might include:

- Current behavioral science encyclopedias or dictionaries
- Recent books in the card catalogue relating to your subject
- Current journals available in the library that cover the topic
- Print indexes such as the *Social Sciences Index* and *Psychological Abstracts*
- Electronic databases

Encyclopedias and Dictionaries

The behavioral science dictionaries and encyclopedias that are usually located in the reference section may be helpful in defining or suggesting related topics to explore. These references may also provide definitions of terms that are keys to accessing the information you want. You may note the date of these publications, realizing that the more current they are, the more useful they will be. For example, the *Thesaurus of Psychological Index Terms* provides descriptor terms that can be useful in subject searches.

Recent Books Relating to Your Subject

Remember that the more recent a book is, the more likely that it uses current advances in psychological theory and methodology. One question you must ask about every book you examine is how sound it is regarding its facts, methods, and findings. Inexperienced researchers, especially, sometimes have trouble determining whether a book is a reliable source of information instead of an untrustworthy compendium of popular but unsubstantiated generalizations. There are a lot of popular self-help books on the market, some of which are academically acceptable, some of which are not. How do you gauge a book's trustworthiness? Here are some tips:

- Determine the level of education and experience of the book's authors. Your source will probably list its authors' academic credentials. You can also check periodical indexes for other publications of your authors as well as for reviews of them.
- Examine the book's reference section. The number and type of reference materials cited will give an indication of how thoroughly the book has been researched.
- Determine whether the book has an index. In addition to making your search for relevant material easier, an index suggests a certain level of professionalism on the part of the authors. Also, browsing through an index can give you a feel for the book's level of professionalism.
- Read quickly any introduction, foreword, or preface; if there is no prefatory text, read the first chapter. Such introductory material can give you a clue not only about the book's purpose, but also about the level of audience to whom the authors address themselves. While it is not always the case, a book obviously intended to perform a self-help service for a particular segment of the popular audience often skimps on the details of its arguments, leaving certain generalizations without documented support.

Finally, remember that if your search for helpful books uncovers titles that are not included among your library's holdings, it is usually possible to obtain the books through the library's interlibrary loan department.

Print Indexes

The reference section of your library will contain several sets of books that index publications in a wide range of fields, including psychology. Here is a brief list of print indexes you might find helpful:

Bibliographic Index. Professional journals often include bibliographies of publications on certain subjects. This index lists such bibliographies and includes many found in psychology periodicals.

Child Development Abstracts. This ongoing work lists contents of professional periodicals and provides book reviews related to child development.

Dissertation Abstracts International. Published in two volumes annually, this mammoth series prints abstracts of dissertations completed in a wide range of fields in universities across the country. Dissertations in psychology are indexed in the second volume under the sciences. Material may be referenced either by keyword in the title or by author. This is another serial index available also by computer.

Index Medicus. Indexing entries by author and subject, this work notes monthly references to articles published in current biomedical periodicals, including psychology journals.

Reader's Guide to Periodical Literature. This series of texts, one volume per year, indexes articles found in a variety of periodicals aimed at the general population rather than at the academic community. Magazine indexes here include *Science, Scientific American* and *Psychology Today.* The *Reader's Guide* includes both an author index and a subject index. It is also available in CD-ROM format.

Social Science Citation Index. This index covers about 1,400 journals in the social sciences, including psychology and psychiatry.

Social Sciences Index. These volumes index the major psychology journals and would be a useful place to start for most introductory psychology papers.

Social Work Research and Abstracts. Its title indicates this series' subject matter and the type of periodicals it covers. It is indexed by author and subject.

Sociological Abstracts. Indexed by author, subject, and source, this project provides brief summaries of texts published in sociology.

Subject Guide to Books in Print. This multivolume, annual publication provides publication information for all nonfiction titles published by a great number of publishing houses. There are separate volumes for authors and for titles.

Electronic Databases

Most libraries by now offer at least a limited number of on-line research database programs. Many of the indexes listed in the section above are available by computer, either through an on-line service or through CD-ROM access. Some on-line search aids have even begun to include complete texts of selected articles along with publication details. Consult with your librarian to determine which electronic programs are available to you.

Many libraries are transferring records of their holdings onto electronic databases accessed by computer terminals. For example, the University of Oklahoma (OU) Catalog is a computerized catalog for the OU Libraries, providing author, title, subject, keyword, and call numbers accessing over 2,300,000 titles owned by the OU Libraries. This catalog includes books, OU theses and dissertations, most periodical titles, government documents (1976–present), and non-book materials. Local researchers may access this on-line catalog by dialing in an access number from a personal computer with a modem. The on-line catalog may also be accessed on the OU Libraries' Web site.

Computer databases can save you a lot of time in the research stage of a project, but remember: It can require an extra degree of skill, flexibility, and imagination to obtain the greatest possible use from these often complicated programs. Be sure to read the operating instructions carefully for each system you use. You do not want to miss finding valuable information in an electronic database simply because you failed to program a search in an acceptable way.

As you search an electronic index such as PSYCLIT®, which is a computerized version of *Psychological Abstracts,* take down the name, date, volume, issue, and page number of each of the articles that seems likely to be of help to you. Then determine if your library owns the journal or magazine by checking the on-line catalog.

Psychology Journals and Other Periodicals

ACTA Psychologica
Advances in Behaviour Research and Therapy
Advances in Developmental Psychology
American Journal of Psychology
American Psychologist
Annals of Theoretical Psychology
Année Psychologique
Annual Review of Psychology
APA Monitor
Archives of Psychology
Australian Journal of Psychology and Philosophy
Australian Journal of Psychology
Behavior and Brain Sciences
Behavior Science
Behavioral Social Sciences Librarian
British Journal of Psychiatry
British Journal of Psychology
British Journal of Psychology General Section
British Journal of Social and Clinical Psychology
British Journal of Statistical Psychology
Bulletin of the Psychonomic Society
Canadian Journal of Experimental Psychology
Canadian Journal of Psychology
Canadian Journal of Psychology/Revue Canadian
Canadian Psychologist/Psychologie Canadienne
Character and Personality
Contemporary Psychology
Contributions to Psychological Theory
Dialectica International Review of Philosophy

Duke University Psychological Monographs
Ethology and Sociobiology
Evolution and Human Behavior Official Journal
Genetic Psychology Monographs
Genetic Social and General Psychology Monographs
Human Behavior
Indian Journal of Psychology
Individual Psychology Bulletin
Integrative Physiological and Behavioral Science
International Journal of Individual Psychology
International Journal of Psychology
Journal de Psychologie Normale et Pathologique
Journal for the Theory of Social Psychology
Journal of Abnormal Psychology
Journal of Applied Psychology
Journal of Consulting and Clinical Psychology
Journal of Consulting Psychology
Journal of Experimental Psychology
Journal of Experimental Research in Personality
Journal of General Psychology
Journal of Genetic Psychology
Journal of Health and Human Behavior
Journal of Health Social Behavior
Journal of Human Development
Journal of Individual Psychology
Journal of Personality
Journal of Philosophy
Journal of Projective Techniques
Journal of Psychological Studies
Journal of Psychology
Journal of Research in Personality
Journal of Russian and East European Psychology
Journal of the Association for the Study of Psychology
Journal of the Experimental Analysis of Behavior
Journal of the History of the Behavioral Sciences
Law Psychology Review
Main Currents in Modern Thought
Merrill Palmer Quarterly Behavior and Development
Mind
Multivariate Experimental Clinical Research
New Directions in Psychology
Newsletter
Pavlovian Journal of Biological Science
Pedagogical Seminary
Personal Growth
Problems of Psychology

Proceedings of the Annual Convention of the American Psychological Association
Professional Psychology
Psychoanalysis
Psychoanalysis and the Psychoanalytic Review
Psychoanalytic Review
Psychoanalytic Review an American Journal of Psychoanalysis
Psychologia
Psychological Bulletin
Psychological Documents
Psychological Exchange
Psychological Newsletter
Psychological Record
Psychological Reports
Psychological Research
Psychological Review
Psychological Science
Psychologische Forschung
Psychology
Psychonomic Science
Readings in Psychology
Revista de Psicologia General y Aplicada
Revista de Psicologia Normal e Patologica
Rorschach Research Exchange
Scandinavian Journal of Psychology
Schweizerische Zeitschrift für Psychologie
Shinrigaku Kenkyu
Soviet Psychology
Studies in Personnel Psychology-Etudes en Psychology
Theoria
Tohoku Psychologica Folia
University of Iowa Studies in Psychology
University of Oregon Monographs Studies in Psychology
Zeitschrift für Experimentelle und Angewandt

6.2 Exercise: Library Research Assignment

The objective of this exercise is for you to improve your skills in finding materials in the library for your psychology writing projects. When you complete this exercise, you should be better able to find the materials you need and cite them appropriately, using APA style, in your paper.

This library research exercise includes five clearly assigned tasks. Specific directions are provided for each task. As you work through the assignment, write your responses on notebook paper. To submit your work to your instructor, type your responses for all five tasks on standard (8½ - by-11-inch) sheets of typing paper. This exercise is a modified version of one developed by Professor Kathleen Donovan at the University of Central Oklahoma.

Task 1. Journals

The following directions apply to the following four journals:

Journal of Counseling and Developmental Psychology
Journal of Clinical Psychology
Journal of Social Psychology
Journal of Experimental Psychology

1. For *each* of the above journals:
   * Locate the most current issue
   * Record the publisher
   * Record the name (s) of the current editor (s)
   * Write a complete and accurate APA-style reference page citation for the first article (see Chapter 4 of this manual).
2. Select an article (one that looks interesting to you) from one of these journals, read it, and write a one-paragraph summary of it. Do not copy the abstract, but write a summary in your own words.

Task 2. Books

Using your library's card catalog (normally a computerized system) find the call numbers for the following four books:

Bandura, A. *Self-efficacy: The exercise of control.*
Skinner, E. *Perceived control, motivation, and coping.*
Gardner, H. *Leading minds: The anatomy of leadership.*
Hunt, Morton. *The story of psychology.*

Task 3. PsychInfo

Ask your librarian for assistance in using an internet connection to access PsychInfo, the automated database for psychology articles. Using PsychInfo, look up the topic of *family violence.* Record in APA style the entire citation for an article that discusses family violence in relation to each of the following populations:

* Children
* Adolescents
* Older women

Next, find the topic heading *schizoid personality* and locate an article about an especially maladjusted well-known murderer. In APA style, type the entire bibliographical citation for that particular article. Finally, locate the following two articles and type the full citation in APA format:

1. Informational feedback and self-esteem among male and female athletes
2. The effects of performance feedback on female self-confidence

Task 4. Psychological Abstracts

Ask your librarian for assistance in locating and using *Psychological Abstracts*. Next, locate the two articles specified below, find printed or microfilm copies of them, and provide the full bibliographical citation for each using APA format:

Buss, D. M. (1984). Toward a psychology of person-environment (PE) correlation: The role of spouse selection.

Stein, L. B., & Brodsky, S. L. (1995). When infants wail: Frustration and gender as variables in distress disclosure.

Task 5. Theses and Dissertations

Students who complete masters and doctorate degrees at your university will probably provide your college library with copies of their theses and dissertations. Locate your college or university's theses and dissertations, if they are available. Select a psychology thesis or dissertation, cite it in APA format and, in two or three sentences, summarize its subject and its goal.

Next, with assistance from your librarian, locate the Comprehensive Dissertation Index of *Dissertation Abstracts International*. Find the Dissertation Title, Volume Number, Issue Number (including the A or B), and Page Number for the thesis or dissertation that was written by your course instructor. With this information, (a) look up the dissertation on microfilm or on a computer, (b) write a one- or two-sentence summary of the abstract, and (c) cite the dissertation in APA style.

7 *The Internet and Distance Learning*

7.1 Writing Resources on the Internet

The preceding chapters of this book have given you much information about research and writing, but the Internet offers even more. A particularly good place to start your search is a World Wide Web site called Researchpaper. com. Created by an Internet publishing company, Researchpaper.com provides free electronic access to a book entitled *10,000 Ideas for Term Papers, Projects, Reports & Speeches.*

Among the links that you will find when you visit Researchpaper.com are these:

- *Idea Directory:* A list of more than 4,000 research topics within over 100 categories. You can type in a key word, and the directory will produce interesting ways of approaching the subject you have chosen.
- *Researchpaper.com Chat:* A "chat room," which is a page where you will find the thoughts and suggestions of other people to whom you can respond.
- *Research Central:* A page that contains help with searching for information and suggestions about good Web sites.
- *Writing Center:* A series of guides to more effective writing, containing ideas for writing techniques and answers to commonly asked questions about grammar and style.

A good place to find help with your writing is at an On-line Writing Lab (OWL). More than seventy colleges and universities have now established OWLs, which offer a wide variety of assistance and information. You may want to begin your OWL search at Purdue University's On-line Writing Lab <http://

owl.english.purdue.edu/>. In addition to a list of other OWLs currently on line, Purdue's OWL home page offers the following information sources for writers of research papers:

- Resources for Writers links, including handouts on topics related to writing, as well as links to other relevant sites
- A collection of search tools and indexes to search the Internet
- Purdue University writing and research resources
- Information about Purdue's Writing Lab
- Indexes for Writers
- On-line reference resources
- Guides to style and editing
- Business and technical writing resources
- Robert Ryan's *Guide to Environmental Writing*
- Alliance for Computers and Writing (ACW)
- Assembly on Computers in English
- The National Writing Centers Association
- The National Writers' Union

Purdue's OWL home page also lists electronic discussion groups, including the Alliance for Computers and Writing, and MegaByte University (MBU) Writing Center.

7.2 Psychology Resources on the Internet

Even large catalogs cannot list all the potential Internet resources for psychology. Our purpose in this chapter is to give you a sample of some of the more interesting sites to show you what you can expect and to whet your appetite for conducting your own search.

So let's take a sample Internet tour—always bearing in mind that the sites you see on your computer screen may have evolved to some degree from the sites described below.

A good place to start your search for psychology resources is the home pages for the major national professional associations whose members practice psychology: the American Psychological Society (APS) and the American Psychological Association (APA).

If you visit the APS home page <http://www.psychologicalscience.org> you will find a list of links that will take you to a variety of other resources. Topics of these links include:

- APS information
- Internet resources
- Teaching resources

- Research resources
- Graduate student resources
- Other psychological societies
- Upcoming psychological conferences
- Research program announcements
- Electronic journals publishers
- Software
- Job search support
- Mental health resources

At the APA's home page <http://www.apa.org/> you will find a link to a site map that provides a similar list. The site map's links include:

- Books
- Consumer Help Center
- Continuing education
- Disaster Response Network
- Graduate Students Organization (APAGS)
- International programs
- Journals
- KidsPsych (Psychology resources related to children)
- *Monitor on Psychology* (APA's monthly magazine)
- Other publications
- PsycCAREERS.com
- PsycINFO (abstracts of over 1,350 scholarly journals)
- PsycLAW (linking psychology and law)
- PsycPORT (news wire service about psychology)
- PsycPractitioner (for practitioners)
- Public interest issues
- Resource Center for Rural Behavioral Health
- Science of psychology
- Teachers of psychology in secondary schools

Another good place to find resources for psychology is Psychweb <http://www.psychweb.com>. Psychweb features a search engine linked to a wide variety of psychology-related Web resources.

The sites described above are only the tip of the Internet psychology iceberg. By following links from these sites you will find literally hundreds of other psychology resources. Once you have begun to explore the Internet, you will discover thousands of sites and dozens of types of information that we have not mentioned in this chapter. Some of the things you will find include:

- *Mailing Lists.* You can join a mailing list and receive by e-mail or in printed form publications of a wide variety of organizations.
- *Bibliographies.* Numerous extensive bibliographies of historical information already appear on the Internet.
- *Publishers and Bookstores.* You will find publishers offering to sell you a copy of virtually any published text on psychology, and you will find bookstores that offer not only new books, but old, outdated, and rare editions of many texts.
- *News Groups.* News groups are Internet pages in which people exchange information on current events.

7.3 The Special Challenges of Distance Learning

Perhaps you are apprehensive about taking a distance learning course, or you want to take one but simply do not know where to begin. In either case, this introduction will help you. You will have some important questions to ask before you sign up, and this section will address some of them.

Are distance learning courses effective? Initial studies indicate that if the amount of material learned is a valid criterion for effectiveness, then the answer is "Yes!" After reviewing more than 400 studies of the effectiveness of distance learning courses, Thomas L. Russell, director emeritus of instructional telecommunications at North Carolina State University, concluded that distance learning and classroom courses were equally effective. This does not mean, however, that the two methods are the same in every respect. Texas Tech psychology professors Ruth S. and William S. Maki found that, when they compared distance learning and classroom introductory psychology courses, distance learning students scored from 5 to 10 percent higher on tests of knowledge but expressed less satisfaction with their courses (Car, 2000). Students in classroom courses appreciated more contact with their professors, and their distance learning counterparts observed that on-line courses required more work than their comparable classroom experiences.

Have no fear. If you are a bit uneasy about taking a course in which your only contact with people will be through e-mail or over the Internet, you have a lot of company. New experiences are almost always a bit unsettling, and you may not be as comfortable with a computer as some of your friends. The good news is that institutions that provide distance learning have gone to a lot of trouble to make your introduction to their courses as trouble-free as possible. When entering their Web sites, you will find easy to follow, step-by-step instructions and sources of help on every aspect of your new education experience.

You may want to visit such a site to see what it is like. A good example is World Campus 101 (WC101), established by Penn State University and located at the following Web address: <www.worldcampus.psu.edu>. (Note that in this chapter, as throughout this manual, Web addresses that appear within the text are enclosed in angle brackets [< >], which are not themselves part of the address.) WC101 is itself a short course that introduces you to Penn State's on-line courses. Presented in five "modules," WC101 covers the following topics, which include virtually everything you would need to know to take an on-line-course:

1. Learning how to be a Penn State World Campus student
2. Using on-line course materials
3. Interacting with your instructor and fellow students
4. Using academic resources in your courses
5. Getting help when you need it

Another good site to visit is <www.onlinelearning.net>, a service of UCLA Extension. This site features answers to a list of commonly asked questions. Reading this material will help you overcome some of your initial trepidation. With respect to UCLA's on-line courses you will find, for example, that UCLA extension on-line courses

- Are open to anyone
- Have specific dates of course initiation and completion
- Require regular printed textbooks
- Can be taken anywhere that an average recent personal computer can operate
- Are accompanied by technical support to help when problems arise
- Are given "asynchronously," which is to say that students are required to send messages frequently to the instructor and other students and can do so at any time of the day or night
- Have actual instructors who do all the same things over the Web site that instructors in classroom courses do
- Have enrollments that are normally limited to twenty students, allowing adequate access to the instructor
- Feature special software that is provided by UCLA Extension, including an on-line orientation to this software

Are you likely to succeed in distance learning courses? The answer to this question depends on a number of factors, and every student will react to distance learning situations at least a little differently than any other. Among the factors that will influence your chances of success, however, are how comfortable and happy you are about

- Working alone
- Communicating with people without seeing them
- Accomplishing tasks without reminders from others
- Using computers
- Solving occasional technical problems on computers
- Learning how to use new software

How is distance learning different from classroom courses? Generally speaking, distance learning and classroom courses are probably more alike than they are different. Like classroom courses, distance learning courses have an actual, living person as an instructor; actual, living people as students; and printed or printable course materials. In both classroom and distance learning, individual initiative and responsibility are required for success, and in both settings the quality of the course depends in large part on the competence of the instructor.

The primary differences are that in distance courses you will work alone on a computer, and you will spend your course-related time according to your own schedule rather than attending classes. While in classroom courses other students and the instructor have a physical presence, in distance learning your contact with others is in electronic form. Interestingly, many students report spending more time on their distance learning courses than on their classroom courses.

Distance learning, therefore, offers several advantages over regular classroom courses. You don't need to commute or relocate. You can sell your car and buy a new freezer, which will afford you several new varieties of frozen pizza. Your distance learning schedule can vary from day to day and week to week. You can connect on a whim or wait until your newborn child awakens you at 2 A.M. and you are unable to get back to sleep. In addition, the interaction with other students in on-line courses is often more satisfying than you might first suspect. As messages start streaming back and forth, each student's personality is revealed. Some students send photos of themselves to give classmates a better idea of who they are.

Now for the down side. There are some disadvantages to on-line learning. The one factor that seems to irritate distance learners most is that they cannot get instant feedback. As a distance learner, you can't just raise your hand and receive an immediate answer to your questions, as you can in a classroom. A related drawback—subtle but profound—is that the nonverbal responses that students unwittingly come to count on in a classroom are missing from an online course. Is your on-line instructor frowning or smiling as she makes a certain comment? In other words, the act of communication is sometimes more complex than we think. Sometimes on-line course instructions are not sufficiently focused or specific, and it may take several communications to understand an assignment.

Another potential difficulty with distance learning is that on-line students are less likely to appreciate options than students in classrooms. Rather than welcome the chance to make their own choices, they tend to want to do exactly what the instructor wants.

Other problems appear in on-line courses occasionally. Sometimes course materials provide ambiguous instructions and out-of-date hyperlinks. Testing can be complicated and may require special passwords. Some students must go to their local community college to take examinations, but other on-line colleges simply remind students of their academic integrity statements.

Some of the disadvantages of distance learning arise from students' personal habits. Staying at home can be fattening if your computer is too close to your refrigerator. If you are social by nature, you may suffer from feelings of isolation. You may find that it takes longer to establish rapport with on-line students with whom you have little in common. There may be some initial confusion as you learn how to run the system and interact effectively, or you may have difficulty interpreting messages from other students. As with your on-line teacher, so with your classmates: Lack of visual contact means a loss of inflection. Humor and sarcasm are more difficult to detect in written communications. And finally, you may face what seems, at times, an overwhelming volume of e-mail featuring a lot of repetition ("Students' Frustrations").

This brief survey of good and bad characteristics of distance learning may help you deal with a range of on-line situations as they arise. All in all, if you assess your own personality correctly, your chances of success in distance learning are substantial.

New distance learning courses are appearing daily. In its second survey of distance-education programs, the U.S. Department of Education identified 1,680 programs in 1998, offering 54,000 on-line courses and enrolling 1.6 million students. These figures represent a 72 percent increase in distance learning activity from 1995 to 1998. The number of psychology courses offered on-line, however, is not extensive. Here are some tips for locating distance learning courses in psychology.

Your local bookstore (as well as <amazon.com> and <barnesandnoble.com>) will offer several guides to distance learning. Among those currently available are:

- *Peterson's Guide to Distance Learning Programs, 2000*
- *Barron's Guide to Distance Learning: Degrees, Certificates, Courses, 1999*
- *College Degrees by Mail & Internet 2000*
- *The Independent Study Catalog*
- *The Best Distance Learning Graduate Schools: Earning Your Degree Without Leaving Home*

Your Internet search for a suitable course may take some time, since offerings change continuously. You can find links to colleges at *Web U.S. Universities, by State* (<www.utexas.edu/world/univ/state/>). You will also find that Western Governors University (<www.wgu.edu>) provides a list of psychology courses available at several other colleges. The list of general distance education resources on the Internet changes almost daily, but some you may want to examine are:

American Distance Education Consortium	www.adec.edu
Chronicle of Higher Education	www.chronicle.com
Distance Education at a Glance	www.uidaho.edu/evo/ distglan.html
Distance Education Clearing House	www.uwex.edu/disted/ home.html
Distance-Educator.com	www.distance-educator.com

International Center for Distance Learning	www-icdl.open.ac.uk
Resources for Distance Education	http://webster.comnet.edu/HP/pages/darling/distance.htm
Web Based Learning Resources Library	www.outreach.utk.cdu/weblearning/
World Lecture Hall	www.utexas.edu/world/lecture/

For Students About to Take or Taking On-Line Courses

Since you have decided to take a distance learning course, decide to study effectively. Studying for distance learning courses requires the same sort of discipline as studying for classroom courses, with one notable difference. For some people, class attendance is energizing. It helps stimulate their desire to study. This stimulus is, of course, absent for distance learners, but e-mail communication with other students and the instructor may serve the same purpose for some. In general, the same study habits that lead to success in regular courses also lead to success in on-line courses. In order to make the point with perhaps a little humor, we have written the following two scenarios about two fictional distance learners, Sidney and Jan.

Sidney spends twenty hours per week studying for his on-line course in animal husbandry. His friends affectionately call his room at the Ticonderoga YMCA "Pompeii," because Sidney's course materials, when they can be found at all, are likely to be located under piles of laundry, empty cereal boxes, or bags of cat litter. Sidney is a night person. His most productive hours, when he is most alert, are from 8 P.M. to 1 A.M. He reserves this "prime time" for playing video games and watching his favorite videos, stacks of which help to keep his floor, except for an occasional few square inches, invisible. Sidney always studies in the morning, when, bleary-eyed, he most enjoys the cacophony created by his electric fan, the television, four parakeets, three cats, and his pet armadillo. Sidney studies sporadically and the morning hours drag on as he anxiously awaits the mail, praying each day for the overdue check from his uncle Rudolph who has promised to fund Sidney's education if Sidney would stay at least fifty miles from Rudolph's home in Casper, Wyoming. When Sidney reads the text for his on-line course, the words all slide through his field of vision without effort and without effect, and he is rarely able to recall content five minutes after it has been perused. Interruptions in study time always take priority, especially when Sidney's friend Morris, who is determined to teach Sidney's cats to play badminton, comes to visit.

Jan is a tank commander in the Israeli army reserve. When she awakens at 5 A.M., her golden retriever, Moshe, delivers the newspaper to her bed, turns on the coffee maker, and sits at attention, awaiting his first command of the day. Jan's most effective hours are in the morning, and three days a week she spends three morning hours concentrating intently on the materials for her on-line course in financial planning. Her Jerusalem condominium is quiet during her study time not only because Jan's only electrical appliances are her coffee maker and microwave oven, but also because her neighbors have learned that life in the neighborhood is much more pleasant if Jan is not disturbed. As she studies, her room floods with morning light, and Jan methodically crosses each successive course requirement off her well-planned list as she accomplishes it.

Sidney and Jan may not be exactly typical students, but you get the idea. To study effectively you must be organized, set aside prime time in a quiet place, and concentrate completely on your study materials.

Australian researcher A. Morgan has identified two approaches that students take to distance learning. Applying the first, less effective method, which Morgan calls the *surface* approach, students "focus on the signs." This is to say that they see the trees rather than the forest. They concentrate on the text or instruction itself rather than on catching the idea or spirit of what is going on. They get stuck on specific elements of the task rather than understanding the whole task. Less effective students like to memorize data, rules, and procedures, which become crutches, substitutes for the more important task of understanding concepts. They also "unreflectively associate concepts and facts," failing to understand how specific facts are related to certain concepts, and therefore getting principles confused with evidence for those principles. Moreover, they consider assignments as mere tasks, or requirements imposed by the instructor, instead of seeing assignments as ways to learn skills or understand concepts that meaningfully relate to the goals of the course or to the realities of life (Morgan, 1991).

As an alternative to this surface approach, Morgan proposes a *deep* approach, in which the student focuses on the concepts being studied and on the instructor's arguments as opposed to the tasks or directions for assignments. The deep approach encourages students to relate new ideas to the real world, to constantly distinguish evidence (data) from argument (interpretations of data), and to organize the course material in a way that is personally meaningful (Morgan).

Researchers Brundage, Keane, and Mackneson have found that successful distance learners are able to:

- Assume responsibility for motivating themselves
- Maintain their own self-esteem irrespective of emotional support that may or may not be gained from the instructor, other students, family, or friends
- Understand accurately their own strengths and limitations and become able to ask for help in areas of weakness
- Take the time to work hard at effectively relating to the other students
- Continually clarify for themselves and others precisely what it is that they are learning and become confident in the quality of their own observations

• Constantly relate the course content to their own personal experience (Brundage, Keane, and Mackneson, 1993)

Good luck in your adventure in distance education. Armed with the information in this introduction, your chances of success are good. One final thought: Studies indicate that the dropout rate for distance learners is higher than for traditional courses. In part this is because distance learners tend to underestimate their other obligations and the time it will take to successfully complete their on-line course. Before you begin, be sure that you allow enough time to not only complete your course, but to do so with a reasonable measure of enjoyment.

Short Writing Assignments for Introduction to Psychology Courses

The short writing assignments in this chapter all have two objectives. The first is to give you practice in writing clearly and concisely. The second objective is to help you formulate your own thoughts on some of the more interesting aspects of psychology. All of the topics in this chapter are discussed in most introductory psychology textbooks, and you may want to read the relevant section of your text for more background information before you begin writing.

8.1 Extrasensory Perception

Many Americans believe in some paranormal phenomenon. For example, one-third of college students believe in reincarnation, and over half believe that dreams have some relevance to prediction of the future. The term *extrasensory perception* (ESP) refers to experiences that occur beyond the senses.

Clairvoyance, telepathy, and precognition are three commonly reported forms of ESP. Clairvoyance is the ability to see objects or events without the use of normal vision. An example of this might be seeing what object is on a card that someone is holding without being shown the card. Joseph Banks Rhine (1895–1980) used Zener cards that contained pictures of either a circle, a cross, a rectangle, a star, or wavy lines. The participants were to guess which picture Rhine was holding without seeing the card. If the participant guessed correctly more than 20 percent of the time—a result that could be obtained by chance—the participant was said to possess a level of clairvoyance. Telepathy is the ability to perceive someone else's thoughts or emotions. In a common experiment to demonstrate telepathy, a receiver (a person expected to receive telepathic information) is placed in a soundproofed room, wearing headphones connected to a receiver playing white noise. Halves of ping pong balls are taped over the receiver's eyes, and a red floodlight is flashed on and off over the ping pong balls. The sender (the person attempting to send a telepathic communication) is in another room and is asked to concentrate on a target. At the end of a thirty-minute trial, the receiver is shown a series of objects and attempts to identify the target. Precognition is the ability to perceive future events before they happen. Psychics like Nostradamus and Jeane Dixon have made some famous predictions, not all of which have been accurate.

In a four- to five-page paper summarize the evidence for and against ESP. Using your textbook, other books, and journal articles, explain what has been reported and actually demonstrated with respect to ESP. In addition, with a friend or fellow student, conduct a simple ESP experiment to see if you exhibit any ESP tendencies. Using a deck of common playing cards, for example, you might have your friend hold up one card at a time (the back of the card facing you) and see if you can identify any of the cards. Evaluate all the evidence and conclude by explaining your own view of the validity of ESP.

8.2 Sensation

Every day we receive an immense amount of sensory information. Much of it comes in the form of sights, sounds, smells, tastes, and vibrations. Many people would say that vision is our most important sense and that our sense of hearing is our next most important sense. But if we suddenly lost our sense of smell or taste, we would quickly realize how much we depend upon it from day to day.

You will begin this assignment by going to a comfortable, familiar, and relatively secluded place. Maybe you know of a nearby park or a stream where you sometimes pause just to take in the beauty of the day. You will need to spend some time there with no distractions. Take a pen and note pad, but leave your cell phone in your room.

Once in this location, your first goal is to relax. If you begin by closing your eyes, you will avoid the common tendency of vision, which is to dominate the other senses. Starting with your sense of smell, write down each sensation you experience. As you advance from smell to hearing to touching to seeing, you will notice a wide variety of things. You may become aware of the different colors of leaves as the sun comes through them or the errant flight of a monarch butterfly. Make your observations as specific and detailed as you can. For example, instead of saying "I saw leaves," you might observe the leaves' motion, color, texture, odor, and contrast to their surroundings.

After making observations for perhaps a half hour to an hour, write a three- to five-page paper in which you describe and comment upon your observations. You might begin by describing the location you chose. You could devote a paragraph or two to each sensation or each phenomenon you observed. Conclude by identifying things you observed in this exercise that you had missed before. You might also talk about ideas for how you might be more observant in the future. For example, how might you take advantage of senses you normally tend to ignore? In terms of vision, how did you see things differently on this occasion than you do normally?

8.3 Development

According to Piaget, a 4-year-old is in the preoperational stage of cognitive development. In other words, 4-year-olds can represent objects with symbols, an activity that allows them to engage in pretend play using dolls, for example, to represent people. They are also egocentric and unable to conceptualize reality from a different point of view. In contrast, a 10-year-old is in the concrete operational stage and can think more logically. A 10-year-old would, therefore, not only be able to think about things symbolically, but also to manipulate symbols, enabling him or her to trade Pokemon cards. Finally, the 10-year-old would also be able to think through problems and come up with solutions for immediate predicaments such as what to do in case of a fire.

The attributes of each stage of development are explained in most introductory psychology texts. Write a five-page essay in which you do three things. First, write a list of instructions for a 4-year-old child on how to accomplish a specific task. For example, your instructions may explain what to do in case of a fire or how to clean up a messy room. The instructions must be in very simple language, the exact language you would use in actually teaching a child how to accomplish the task you have selected. Second, write a set of instructions that would teach a 10-year-old how to do the same task. Third, explain the differences in the two lists of instructions you have created and explain why your first list is developmentally appropriate for a 4-year-old, while your second list is developmentally appropriate for a 10-year-old.

9 Critical Examination of Psychological Literature

9.1 Article Critiques

An *article critique* is a paper that evaluates an article published in an academic journal. A good critique tells the reader what point the article is trying to make and how convincingly it makes this point. Writing an article critique achieves three purposes. First, it provides you with an understanding of the information contained in a scholarly article. Second, it provides an opportunity to apply and develop your critical thinking skills as you attempt to evaluate a psychologist's work. Third, it helps you to improve your own writing skills as you attempt to describe the selected article's strengths and weaknesses so that your readers can clearly understand them.

Preparing to Write an Article Critique

The first step in writing an article critique is to select an appropriate article. Unless your instructor specifies otherwise, select an article from a scholarly journal, such as the *American Psychologist,* the *Journal of Counseling Psychology,* or the *Journal of Consulting and Clinical Psychology,* and not a popular or journalistic publication, such as *Time* or *Psychology Today.* Chapter 6 of this manual includes a substantial list of academic psychology journals, but your instructor may also accept appropriate articles from academic journals in other disciplines.

The second step is to browse titles in the journal until you find a topic that interests you. Writing a critique will be much more satisfying if you have an interest in the topic. Hundreds of interesting journal articles are published every year. The following articles, for example, appeared in a single issue (January 2000) of the journal *American Psychologist* (Vol. 55, Number 1), a special issue dedicated to the concept of happiness:

- "Positive Psychology: An Introduction," by Martin E-P. Seligman and Mihaly Csikszentmihalyi
- "The Evolution of Happiness," by David M. Buss
- "Individual Development in a Bio-Cultural Perspective," by Fausto Massimini and Antonella Delle Fave
- "Subjective Well-Being: The Science of Happiness and a Proposal for a National Index," by Ed Diener
- "The Future of Optimism," by Christopher Peterson
- "The Funds, Friends, and Faith of Happy People," by David G. Myers
- "Self-Determination Theory and the Facilitation of Intrinsic Motivation, Social Development, and Well-Being," by Richard M. Ryan and Edward L. Deci
- "Self-Determination: The Tyranny of Freedom," by Barry Schwartz
- "Adaptive Mental Mechanisms: Their Role in a Positive Psychology," by George E. Vaillant
- "Psychological Resources, Positive Illusions, and Health," by Shelley E. Taylor, Margaret E. Kemeny, Geoffrey M. Reed, Julienne E. Bower, and Tara L. Gruenewald
- "Emotional States and Physical Health," by Peter Salovey, Alexander J Rothman, Jerusha B. Detweiler and Wayne T. Steward
- "Wisdom: A Metaheuristic (Pragmatic) to Orchestrate Mind and Virtue Toward Excellence," by Paul B. Baltes and Ursula M. Staudinger

Besides picking an article of interest to you, another consideration in selecting an article is your current level of knowledge. Many psychology students are not knowledgeable about sophisticated statistical techniques. You may be better prepared to evaluate a sophisticated statistical procedure if you have studied statistics.

Finally, it may be helpful to pick an article that has been written within the last twelve months. The reason for this is that most material in psychology is quickly superseded by new studies. Selecting a recent article will help insure that you will be engaged in a current discussion of your topic.

The Components of an Article Critique

Now that you have selected your article, the third step is to read your article carefully and begin to write your critique. This critique will consist of five parts:

1. Thesis
2. Methods

3. Evidence of Thesis Support
4. Contribution to the Literature
5. Recommendation

Thesis

The first task is to state the thesis of the article clearly and succinctly. The thesis is the main point of the article. Here is the introduction from an article by Reed W. Larson, psychologist at the University of Illinois at Urbana-Champagne, entitled "Toward a Psychology of Positive Youth Development," published in the January 200 issue of the *American Psychologist* (pp. 170–183). Can you tell which sentence in this introduction is capable of operating as a thesis sentence—in other words, the sentence that determines the direction that the paper will take?

It cannot be said, as for other domains of psychology, that developmental psychology has neglected the positive. Development, after all, is a process of growth and increasing competence. In the important subdomain of social and emotional development, however, we are often more articulate about how things go wrong than how they go right. We have a burgeoning field of developmental psychopathology but have a more diffuse body of research on the pathways whereby children and adolescents become motivated, directed, socially competent, compassionate, and psychologically vigorous adults. Corresponding to that, we have numerous research-based programs for youth aimed at curbing drug use, violence, suicide, teen pregnancy, and other problem behaviors, but lack a rigorous applied psychology of how to promote positive youth development.

The place for such a field is apparent to anyone who has had contact with a cross section of American adolescents. In such a group, one encounters a surprising number of youth who appear to be bored, unmotivated, and unexcited about their lives. This malaise was brought home to me when we obtained a random sampling of self-reports on 16,000 moments in the daily experience of a representative sample of White, working- and middle-class young adolescents—a group that seemingly has everything going for them. These youth reported feeling bored for 27% (4,300!) of these random moments (Larson & Richards, 1991). Of course, individuals differed in these rates, but what was surprising was that honor students were as likely as those involved in delinquent activities to be among those reporting high rates of boredom, in many cases for more than 50% of the random moments. The litany of explanations for this boredom—"algebra sucks," "I'm always bored on Sunday . . . there's nothing to do," "the Odyssey is boring"—reads like a script from Bart Simpson. They communicate an ennui of being trapped in the present, waiting for someone to prove to them that life is worth living.

High rates of boredom, alienation, and disconnection from meaningful challenge are not signs of psychopathology, at least not in most cases, but rather signs of a deficiency in positive development. The same might be said for many cases of problem behavior, such as drug use, premature sexual involvement, and minor delinquency that they are more parsimoniously described, not as responses to family stress, emotional disturbance, or maladaptive cognitions, but rather to the absence of engagement in a positive life trajectory. Many youth do their schoolwork, comply with their parents, hang out with their friends, and get through the day, but are not invested in paths into the future that excite them or feel like they originate from within. A central question of youth development is how to get adolescents' fires lit, how to have them develop the complex of dispositions and skills needed to take charge of their lives. This calling is made particularly difficult by the absence of a well-developed body of relevant theory and research regarding these dispositions and skills.

In this article, I am going to focus on adolescents' development of initiative, which I see as a core quality of positive youth development in Western culture. The construct *initiative* is closely related to capacity for agency or for autonomous action that others have discussed (Brandtstadter, 1998; Deci, 1995; Ryan, 1993). It consists of the ability to be motivated from within to direct attention and effort toward a challenging goal. In addition to being an important quality in its own right, I believe that initiative is a core requirement for other components of positive development, such as creativity, leadership, altruism, and civic engagement. (p. 170)

The last sentence in the paragraph states the thesis of the article, which is that initiative is essential to positive development of adolescents. Many authors, however, do not present their thesis this clearly, despite the crucial importance of doing so. Do you have to hunt for the thesis of the article you are critiquing? Comment in your critique about the clarity of the author's presentation and state the author's thesis in your own paper. Before proceeding with the remaining elements of your paper, consider the importance of the topic. Have the authors written something that is important for us as citizens or psychologists to read?

Methods

What methods did the authors use to investigate the topic? In other words, how did the authors go about supporting their thesis? In your critique, carefully answer the following questions:

1. Were appropriate methods used? (Did the authors' approach to supporting their thesis make sense?)
2. Did the authors employ their selected methods correctly? (Did you discover any errors in the way they conducted their research?)

No matter how professionally a published article is structured and written, there is usually an element or two that could have used some improvement. For example, in the study by Richie, et al., entitled "Persistence, Connection, and Passion: A Qualitative Study of the Career Development of Highly Achieving African American Black and White Women," published in volume 44 of the *Journal of Counseling Psychology,* 125 nationally prominent, highly successful African American women were questioned by survey. For the final study, a matched sample of African American women were included to explore the effects of both racism and sexism on career development.

One of the methodological problems with this study is that it was based on one in-depth interview with each woman. Additional sources such as information from diaries, archival documents, or observations might have strengthened the study. Moreover, the sample consisted only of women in the Northeast who were similar in age and developmental phase of life. It may be important, therefore, to test this model with samples representative of other populations. For example, Rainey and Border's (1997) inclusion of a group of rural, adolescent girls and their mothers and the cultural diversity of Lucas's (1997) sample are examples of how alternative samples might strengthen the generalized conclusions of the Richie et al., study.

Evidence of Thesis Support

In your critique, answer the following questions:

- What evidence did the authors present in support of the thesis?
- What are the strengths of the evidence presented?
- What are the weaknesses of the evidence presented?
- On balance, how well did the authors support their thesis?

Focusing on finding answers to these questions can help you to determine the organization not only of the paper but also of the research on which the paper was based. For example, in order to write an article critique, a student applied these questions to a 1997 study by Lochner and Melchert, "Relationship of Style and Theoretical Orientation to Psychology Interns' Preferences for Supervision," published in volume 44 of the *Journal of Counseling Psychology*. The student determined that the essay's goal was to study preferences among beginning and advanced psychotherapy students for certain types of professional supervision. By keeping the questions above in mind, the student was able to determine the essay's methodology: Lockner and Lelchert hypothesized that students at a lower level of professional development usually prefer a more task-oriented, behaviorally structured style of supervision, while more advanced students, in contrast, prefer a more interpersonal style of supervision that is less structured. The essay's thesis was that interns whose orientations were more behavioral preferred supervisors who were more task oriented, and interns who were more psychoanalytic-psychodynamic, humanistic, or experiential preferred supervisors who were more interpersonal.

In determining the article's strengths, the student writing the critique found that the researchers applied a correlational analysis to over 100 students. In suggesting possible weaknesses in support of the thesis, the student noted that it might not be accurate to assume, as the essay implies, that student development is enhanced by providing trainees with what is most comfortable or familiar to them. In her critique the student suggestion that some concrete measures of positive training outcome might need to be considered in future research.

Contribution to the Literature

This step will probably require you to undertake some research. Using the research resources discussed in Chapters 6 and 7, identify articles and books published within the last five years on the subject of your selected article. Browse the titles and read perhaps a half dozen of the publications that appear to provide the best discussion of the topic. In your critique, list the most important of these articles or books that have been published on your topic, and then, with these publications in mind, evaluate the contribution that your selected article makes to a better understanding of its topic.

For example, a 1997 article by Hill, Diemer, and Heaton entitled "Dream Interpretation Sessions: Who Volunteers, Who Benefits, and What Volunteer Clients View as Most and Least Helpful," published in volume 44 of the *Journal of Counseling Psychology*, attempts to determine if dream interpretation is viewed as being helpful. A researcher preparing an article critique of this essay would look for previously published work on the topic of dream interpretation. A satisfactory search would find, among other things, that previous studies have attempted to address the question of what type of people volunteer for dream interpretation studies (Cogar & Hill, 1992; Falk & Hill, 1995; Rosenthall and Rosnow, 1996). Reading through these studies, our researcher would discover that the information in the 1997 Hill, Diemer, and Heaton article actually connects with findings in the earlier studies, in that it attempts to obtain information about those people who volunteer for dream interpretations but who fail to participate.

In addition, previous studies have found no correlation between visualizer-verbalizer dimension, psychological mindedness, and responsiveness to dream interpretations (Cogar & Hill, 1992; Diemer et al., 1996). The Hill, Diemer, and Heaton study looked at other measures of cognitive functioning that are supposed to be related to ability to benefit from dream interpretations, such as the ability to recall dreams, the ability to maintain a positive attitude towards dreams, the ability to visualize dreams, and the ability to process cognitive complexity.

Finally, the Hill et al. study also collected anecdotal information asking the clients open-ended questions about what was either helpful or not helpful about the dream interpretations sessions themselves. The writer of the article critique was able to pass on this information about the essay's contribution to the literature of dream interpretation only by first examining that literature.

Recommendation

In this section, summarize your evaluation of the article clearly, answering the following questions for your reader:

- Who will benefit from reading this article?
- What will the benefit be?
- How important and extensive is that benefit?

Here is a paragraph from the recommendation section of a critique of a 1996 article by Humphreys entitled "Clinical Psychologists as Psychotherapists: History, Future, and Alternatives," published in volume 44 of the *American Psychologist:*

> In summary, Humphreys adequately supports his conclusion that psychologists are being replaced by lower cost, masters-level providers. This article would have a broad based appeal not only for providers of psychotherapy but also for anyone else attempting to access the mental health care delivery system. The primary benefit of this article is the detail with which it describes the context of the current political-economic circumstances in order to explain why psychologists are being priced out of the market of psychotherapy. The problem with this article is that the job alternatives it suggests for out-of-work psychologists, such as going into consultation or education, may not be realistic.

When writing your critique, follow the directions for formats in Chapter 3. Ask your instructor for directions concerning the length of the paper, but in the absence of further directions, your paper should not exceed five typed, double spaced pages.

9.2 How to Conduct a Literature Review

Your goal in writing a research paper is to provide your readers an opportunity to increase their understanding of the subject you are addressing. They will want the most current and precise information available. Whether you are writing a traditional library research paper or conducting an experiment, you must know what has already been learned in order to give your readers comprehensive and up-to-date information or to add something new to what is already known about the subject. If your topic is the attributes of depression, for example, you will want to find out precisely what attributes of depression have already been identified by people who have done depression research. When you seek this information, you will be conducting a literature review, which is a thoughtful collection and analysis of available information on the topic you have selected for study. It tells you, before you begin your experiments or analyses, what is already known about the subject.

Why do you need to conduct a literature review? It would be embarrassing to spend a lot of time and effort preparing a study, only to find that the information you are seeking has already been discovered by someone else. Also, a properly conducted literature review will tell you many things about a particular subject. It will tell you the extent of current knowledge, sources of data for your research, examples of what is not known about the subject (which generates ideas for formulating hypotheses), methods that have been used for research, and clear definitions of concepts relevant to your own research.

Let us consider an example. Suppose that you have decided to research the question: "How will depressed adolescents express their depression in their relationships with their friends?" First, you will need to establish a clear definition of "depression," then you will need to find a way to identify the ways in which depressed adolescents relate with their friends. Using techniques explained in this and other chapters of this manual, you will begin your research by looking for studies that address your research question or similar questions at the library, on the Internet, and through other resources. You will discover that many studies have been written on adolescents and depression. As you read these studies, certain patterns will appear. Some research methods will appear to have produced better results than others. Some studies will be quoted in others many times—some confirming and others refuting what previous studies have done. You will constantly be making choices as you examine these studies, reading very carefully ones that are highly relevant to your purposes, and skimming those of only marginal interest. As you read, constantly ask yourself the following questions:

- How much is known about this subject?
- What is the best available information, and why is it better than other information?
- What research methods have been used successfully in relevant studies?
- What are the possible sources of data for further investigation of this topic?
- What important information is still not known, in spite of all previous research?
- Of the methods that have been used for research, which are the most effective for making new discoveries? Are new methods needed?
- How can the concepts being researched be more precisely defined?

You will find that this process, like the research process as a whole, is recursive: Insights related to one of the above questions will spark new investigations into others, and these investigations will then bring up a new set of questions, and so on.

Your instructor may request that you include a literature review as a section of the paper that you are writing. Your written literature review may be from one to several pages in length, but it should always answer these questions:

1. What specific previously compiled or published studies, articles, or other documents provide the best available information on the selected topic?
2. What do these studies conclude about the topic?
3. What are the apparent methodological strengths and weaknesses of these studies?
4. What remains to be discovered about the topic?
5. What appear to be, according to these studies, the most effective methods for developing new information on the topic?

The success of your own research project depends in large part on the extent to which you have carefully and thoughtfully answered these questions.

10 Traditional (Nonexperimental) Psychology Research Papers

10.1 An Introduction to Traditional Papers in Psychology

The word *traditional* does not have a fixed or precise meaning in psychology today, but it is commonly employed to describe research papers that do not directly employ the experimental methods described in Chapter 11 of this manual. Traditional research papers are studies that clearly describe a particular psychologist, concept, behavior, or method without actually conducting experiments or surveys. While traditional papers may discuss the results and methods of experimental studies, they normally do so to synthesize knowledge learned from a variety of experimental and theoretical sources.

10.2 Steps in Writing a Traditional Paper

When writing your traditional psychology paper, follow the structural and procedural suggestions that are found in Chapters 1 through 7. Traditional papers may be written on many subjects and may emphasize different aspects of these subjects. *Be sure to ask your instructor to clarify the assignment.* Several basic steps, however, must be taken in order to write any traditional paper. Since all of these steps are described in detail in Chapters 1 through 7 of this manual, only specific additional comments will be made here. The seven specific steps to be taken in writing a traditional paper are:

1. Select a topic.
2. Narrow the topic.
3. Conduct preliminary research.
4. Develop a hypothesis.
5. Conduct intensive research.
6. Clearly identify a thesis.
7. Support the thesis.

Selecting a Topic

Topics for traditional papers in psychology may come from all areas of the discipline. Before beginning your search, read the guidelines for selecting a topic presented in Chapter 1. *Ask your instructor for specific advice on what is an appropriate topic for the course.* Traditional college research papers in psychology attempt to help readers understand many aspects of psychology, but they normally discuss a topic selected from one of the following general areas:

- Contributors to psychology
- Psychological constructs
- Psychological disorders
- Methods of psychological research and therapy
- Specialties and subfields of psychology

Papers that discuss contributors to psychology select a prominent psychologist or someone else (an anthropologist, sociologist, biologist) who has made a contribution to the study of psychology, and then focus upon a particular aspect of that person's work. Among the many people who have made fascinating contributions to psychology are the following:

Alfred Adler	Milton Erikson	Heinz Hartman
Eric Berne	Erik Erikson	Karen Horney
Alfred Binet	Sigmund Freud	Abraham Maslow
Leland Bradford	Anna Freud	Carl Rogers
David Buss	Eric Fromm	Hermann Rorschach
Rudolph Dreikers	William Glasser	Harry Stack Sullivan
Albert Ellis	G. Stanley Hall	David Wechsler

Another group of topics for traditional papers consists of what are known as *psychological constructs,* that is, theories and concepts that are widely used in the discipline. Some constructs, such as *authenticity,* have generally recognized definitions in addition to special meanings for psychologists. Examples of psychological constructs are:

acceptance	desensitization	nonverbal behavior
active listening	diagnosis	Oedipus complex
addiction	displacement	oral stage
anal stage	dissociation	personality
anchoring	ego	phallic stage
anecdotal evidence	Electra complex	phenomenal field
authenticity	empty chair technique	phobia
beliefs	encounter groups	placebo effect
birth order	fixation	projection
bisexuality	genital stage	reaction formation
body image	id	reality
boundaries	identification	regression
burnout	instinct	reinforcement
conditioning	integration	repression
cognition	introjection	self-concept
compensation	intuition	shame
congruence	latency stage	somatization
conscience	libido	sublimation
countertransference	memory	superego
denial	motivation	unconscious
depression	neurosis	

Psychological disorders, or impediments to mental health, are a third group of possible topics. You will find a wide variety of disorders described in the latest edition of *Diagnostic and Statistical Manual of Mental Disorders* (Washington, DC: American Psychiatric Press), including the following:

adjustment disorders	disruptive behaviors	identity disorder
agoraphobia	dissociation	insomnia
autism	dyssomnia	kleptomania
bulimia	dysthymia	malingering
compulsion	exhibitionism	masochism
cyclothymia	fetishism	mental retardation
delusion	frotteurism	narcissism
dementia	hallucinosis	obsession
dependence	histrionic personality	panic disorder
depression	hypersomnia	paranoia

paraphilia   psychosis   stress

parasomnia   pyromania   stuttering

pedophilia   schizophrenia   substance abuse

phobia   schizotypal personality Tourette's disorder

post-traumatic   senility   transsexualism
stress disorder

Methods of psychological research and therapy constitute another group of topics for traditional papers in psychology. Some of the common methods of psychological research and therapy are:

analogue studies   electroconvulsive therapy   psychoanalysis

behavioral counseling   existential therapy   rational-emotive
                                                            therapy
case studies   experiments

correlational studies   gestalt therapy   reality therapy

cross-cultural studies   person-centered   transactional
                               therapy   analysis
descriptive psychopathology

The final set of topics for traditional papers includes *specialties and subfields of psychology*. Some of the most prominent areas of study for psychologists are

adult development   humanistic psychology   psychological study of
                                                            women
applied experimental   media psychology
   psychology   psychology of art
                            military psychology
clinical psychology   psychology of religion
                            neuropsychology
comparative psychology   psychology of women
                            neuroscience
consulting psychology   rehabilitation
                            organizational psychology   psychology
consumer psychology
                            peace psychology   school psychology
counseling psychology
                            psychoanalysis   social psychology
developmental psychology
                            psychological study of   sport psychology
educational psychology   ethnic minority issues
                                                        theoretical and
engineering psychology   psychological study of   philosophical
                               lesbian and gay issues   psychology
environmental psychology
                            psychological study of
experimental psychology   men and masculinity

family psychology

health psychology

Narrow the Topic

All of the suggested topics in the above lists have been described in dozens if not hundreds of publications. Each one is too broad by itself for a college traditional paper, because it would take many more than twenty pages of writing simply to describe them adequately. Suggestions for narrowing the topic are explained in more detail in Chapter 1 of this manual, but here is a chart that includes some suggestions for how to narrow some of the topics for traditional papers listed above:

BROAD TOPIC	NARROWED TOPIC
Erik Erikson	Erikson's eight stages of human development
Carl Rogers	Original features of Roger's contributions to psychology
depression	the relationship of light to depression
phobia	fear of embarrassment
bulimia	special features of bulimia in men
senility	senility and diet
cross-cultural studies	prevalence of psychological disorders in Bolivia and Japan
reality therapy	results of reality therapy with female adolescents
military psychology	the effects of basic training on creativity
psychology of art	Picasso's blue period

Conduct Preliminary Research

To conduct preliminary research, first discuss the topic with your instructor. Next, find one or two articles or books that summarize, in a general way, the current knowledge on your topic.

Develop a Hypothesis

After reading a summary of the current literature, and before proceeding to more research, establish a *working hypothesis*. In other words, form an educated guess about an aspect of the subject that interests you. If your general topic is phobia, and your narrowed topic is fear of embarrassment, your hypothesis might be: "Fear of embarrassment is caused by a primary childhood social trauma."

Conduct Intensive Research

Your next step is to dig deeply into the literature. looking for evidence that confirms or disconfirms your hypothesis. If the available evidence seems to contradict your hypothesis, do not ignore it! Continue your investigation. If you decide that current evidence is weak and inconclusive, continue to support your hypothesis. If the current evidence is convincing, change your hypothesis to conform to the evidence.

Clearly Identify a Thesis

Once you have accepted your hypothesis and found sufficient evidence to confirm it, it becomes the thesis of your article. *Take care in the crafting of your thesis sentence,* because it will direct the course of your paper.

Support the Thesis

After you have clearly stated your thesis, the rest of your paper should consist of a careful, logical presentation of evidence that supports the thesis.

10.3 The Elements of a Traditional Paper

Traditional papers in psychology should have

* A title page
* A body
* Source citations in the text and a reference page

Chapters 3 and 4 provide formats for all three elements. The body of your text should contain four components. First, your introduction, often no longer than a paragraph, should clearly describe the subject of the paper and state its thesis. Second, you should provide some background information that will help orient the reader to the subject. For example, if you are writing about a topic in existential therapy, you should include a one- or two-page summary of the history of the development of existential therapy and its primary principles and procedures.

Third, provide a clear and logical defense of your thesis, using as much evidence as you can from studies found in the literature. Be honest. Do not overlook significant objections to your thesis, but confront them with an explanation of your reasons for their weaknesses. Finally, conclude your paper with a summary of the major arguments for accepting your thesis.

11 Experimental Research Papers

11.1 The Fundamentals of Scientific Inquiry in the Discipline of Psychology

Psychology is an empirical science. This means that psychologists seek knowledge by accepting as true only those statements that are supported by evidence that can be tested in scientific experiments. To discover a new fact or truth, psychologists first construct a *hypothesis,* a statement that defines a relationship between two variables, and then they collect evidence to determine whether the hypothesis is true. *Variables* are things that affect or are affected by other things. While a chemist may be interested in the relationship between such variables as temperature and oxidation, psychologists test variables of human cognition, emotion, and behavior, such as learning capacity, anger, stress, procrastination, aggression, or smoking. A psychologist's hypothesis, for example, might therefore be: "Smoking reduces stress," "Depression may be caused by lack of sunlight," or "Antisocial behavior may be diminished by establishing trust with authority figures."

To test hypotheses, psychologists often use *experiments,* controlled situations that allow researchers to determine the relationship between two variables by eliminating the effects of other variables. For example, suppose that an experimenter wants to determine the effect of noise on levels of anxiety. She could measure the levels of anxiety of a selected group of people, then either increase or decrease the noise level to which they are subjected, and finally measure the level of anxiety again. During this process, however, she will need to eliminate other variables that may affect the subjects' anxiety level, such as delays in beginning the experiment, or prolonged disruptive influences during the experiment.

Psychologists have specific names for the variables within an experiment. The variable that is being affected (in our example, the subjects' level of anxiety) is the *dependent variable*. The variable creating the effect (the noise level) is the *independent variable*. *Control variables* are those variables that the experimenter wants to eliminate or control. Control variables may be either *antecedent variables,* which occur before the independent variable is applied (such as delays in starting the experiment), or *intervening variables,* which occur after the independent variable has been introduced (for example, disturbances during the experiment).

Experiments have produced a vast store of knowledge for psychologists. Consider two famous examples. In 1901 Russian psychologist Ivan Pavlov (1849–1936) conducted an experiment that demonstrated that dogs could be made to salivate by ringing a bell. In his experiment, he first repeatedly gave dogs food at the sound of a bell and then eventually he rang the bell without offering food. When the dogs heard the bell, they began to salivate in anticipation of the food, even though no food was offered. This experiment led to Pavlov's development of the concept of *classical conditioning*. In other experiments Pavlov demonstrated that classical conditioning also applies to people in a multitude of ways. For example, a person who once in her childhood ate too much butter and became ill might for the rest of her life begin to feel nauseated whenever she thinks of butter. This person has been "conditioned" to dislike butter.

A second example of an experiment is drawn from the work of Yale Professor Stanley Milgram. In a controversial experiment conducted in the early 1960s, Milgram proved that normally ethical people could be induced to comply with immoral demands by authority figures. Volunteers in Milgram's experiments were told to give other people painful electrical shocks as punishment for making mistakes in assigned tasks. The volunteers were unaware that the recipients of the shocks were actually confederates (people who assist in experiments, following the experimenter's directions) and that, in reality, no shocks were being delivered. Even though the volunteers believed their victims were in extreme pain, most of them continued to administer the shocks simply because they were urged to do so by authority figures. Of forty volunteers, only five refused to deliver the most painful shocks. Another interesting fact is that not one of the volunteers reported the nature of the experiments to the university. Milgram's experiment provided researchers with disturbing data about the complex relationship between the human tendency to obey authority and the needs of the human conscience.

Eliminating extraneous (unwanted) variables from an experiment is almost always a difficult task. What has become known as the *Hawthorne effect* is a famous example of how control variables can affect an experiment's results. In an early effort to improve employee productivity, the Western Electric Company in 1927 conducted experiments to determine if better lighting increased employee morale. To their surprise, the experimenters found that morale improved when they either increased or decreased the amount of light available to employees. What they discovered after further investigation was that the employees responded not to changes in light, but to the fact that management cared about morale enough to test changes in their environment. Because employees interpreted the experiment as a sign of concern for their welfare, the very fact that an experiment was being conducted became an intervening variable in the study! The *Hawthorne effect* is one of the most famous of phenomena known generally as *experimenter effects,* in which things that experimenters do inadvertently affect the results of the experiment.

In addition to experimenter effects, psychologists must consider the ethical implications of their actions. Before conducting experiments, students should read *Ethical Principles of Psychologists and Code of Conduct* (Copyright © 1992 American Psychological Association), which is reprinted by permission in Chapter 12 of this manual. Here are some of the most important ethical rules to follow:

- Use accepted instruments and procedures.
- Do not falsify data.
- Take special care to prevent the common experimenter pitfalls.
- Obtain proper permission to conduct an experiment, approved by your professor and/or your school's institutional review board (IRB).
- Draft and use appropriate consent forms for researcher and participant protection.
- Seek assistance when you have doubts.
- Do no harm to research subjects.

11.2 Steps in Writing an Experimental Research Paper

Writing an experimental research paper requires the researcher to complete six basic tasks:

1. Define a problem or issue.
2. Develop a testable hypothesis.
3. Design the experiment.
4. Conduct the experiment.
5. Analyze the data.
6. Report the findings.

Step 1: Define a Problem or Issue

The world is full of problems and issues of interest to psychologists. You may find them in your own or friends' behaviors, in newspapers, on television, at the supermarket, or at the bowling alley. The key to a highly successful experimental research paper is to study something that interests you. An excellent way to find a good topic is to select a particular day of the week on which to be particularly observant of the world around you. Take notes at every possible moment during the day. Notice the simple things going on around you. Make observations. Your list might include entries that look something like this:

```
    My roommate Janice always brushes her teeth with exactly 32 strokes
of the toothbrush.
    When the plane lands, all the passengers immediately stand up in the
aisles, even though they always have to wait at least ten minutes before
the door opens.
    Professor Smolniakinski always mispronounces my name. I'm Jennifer,
not Hennifer!
    The librarian refuses to make change for the copy machine.
    The vice president used the word "implementation" 33 times in his
presentation.
    Garth blows smoke rings out his nose.
    Jerry likes red and rock music. I like blue and slow jazz.
```

After taking notes for a while, you may find that you are naturally interested in people's preferences in music and their reactions to colors. You wonder: "Can music influence a person's choice of colors?"

Step 2: Develop a Testable Hypothesis

As we noted previously, a hypothesis is a statement that defines a relationship between two variables. Continuing with our example, you might form an initial hypothesis:

```
Color preferences are affected by music.
```

This statement has the basic elements of a good hypothesis. It has a dependent variable (color preferences) and an independent variable (music). But this hypothesis is actually too broad. As it is stated, it covers all people, places, and times. Proving this hypothesis is too much for an elementary experiment. You then try to narrow the hypothesis so that you can realistically construct an experiment that might test it:

```
Research subjects exposed to hard rock music will tend to
select bright and strong colors, whereas research subjects
exposed to easy listening music will be more likely to se-
lect soft colors.
```

This hypothesis appears to be testable in a modest experiment.

Step 3: Design the Experiment

Experiments may be designed in dozens of ways, and you will need to consult with your instructor to determine if your design is appropriate for your hypothesis. Many simple experiments, however, will follow the procedures described in our example. To design your experiment you will need to:

1. Select subjects.
2. Establish experimental and control groups.
3. Design the experimental activity.
4. Design the data collection and analysis procedures.

In order to generate results that reflect patterns in the general population, you would need to conduct a random sample. Random sample procedures vary according to the project, and if you decide to conduct one, your instructor will give you specific instructions. For the purposes of an introductory exercise in experimentation, a *convenience sample,* which uses subjects easily available, is adequate. It will probably be most convenient to have your fellow classmates be your subjects if your experiment concerns other people. If your class is to be your sample population, an easy way to divide it into groups randomly is to write the students' names on pieces of paper and draw them out of a hat, selecting every other name for your experimental and control groups, respectively.

Your experimental activity must clearly test your hypothesis. Since in our example we want to see if choice of music affects choice of color, our experimental design will involve three groups of students. We shall have them meet at the same time in three different rooms. All students will be provided twelve crayons (six bright or fluorescent colors and six pastel tones) and a sheet of paper. All three groups will be given ten minutes to draw a picture. Since different subjects for the pictures (for example, vacation, family, weather) may generate different emotions for different people, all three groups will be asked to draw the same still-life composition of common items. While each group is drawing, hard rock music will be played for the first group, easy listening music for the second group, and no music at all for the third group.

To analyze the data, we shall minimize differing interpretations by having one person (the student conducting the experiment) analyze all the pictures. For each drawing, the student will estimate the percentage of the drawing that has utilized bright colors, and the percentage of the drawing that has utilized soft colors. The student researcher will then construct a data presentation table that includes the following items:

	Number of participants	Mean percentage of bright colors per participant	Standard deviation of bright colors per group
Group 1: Rock music			
Group 2: Easy listening music			
Group 3: No music			
Total: All three groups			

Please note that this table provides only for determining means and standard deviations for each group. Consult your instructor for directions concerning which statistics to use and how to calculate them.

Step 4: Conduct the Experiment

Follow your research design as carefully as possible in conducting your experiment.

NOTE. Most colleges and universities have policies concerning research with human subjects, even in classroom activities. Sometimes administrative offices known as *institutional review boards* (IRBs) are established to review research proposals to ensure that the rights of human subjects are protected. It may be necessary for you to obtain permission, either from such a board or from your college, to conduct your survey. *Be sure to comply with all policies of your university with respect to research with human subjects.*

Step 5: Analyze the Data

Your data analysis techniques should carefully follow your research design.

Step 6: Report the Findings

See the following section for an example of how to present findings.

11.3 Elements of an Experimental Research Paper

According to the guidelines established by the American Psychological Association, experimental research papers are composed of five basic elements:

1. Title page
2. Abstract
3. Text
    a. Introduction
    b. Literature review
    c. Method
    d. Results
    e. Discussion
4. Reference page
5. Appendices

The information given in Chapters 1 through 5 about how to research, structure, draft, revise, and complete a research paper are relevant to the kind of assignment we have been discussing here.

12 *Professional Ethics for Psychologists*

Throughout their careers psychologists, in their roles as therapists, researchers, teachers, administrators, or consultants, confront many situations that raise questions of ethics. Before proceeding with the requirements of a writing assignment, we shall briefly consider an area of ethical concern to psychologists that has received considerable recent public attention: the delayed memory debate.

12.1 Delayed Memory: A Possible Pitfall

The therapist-client relationship provides the setting for many potential ethical problems. Clients are usually distressed and look to their therapists for help, support, and encouragement. Much of the success of therapy depends upon the creation of a relationship of trust involving intimately personal matters, and the client can become vulnerable to the therapist's influence. Not only is it possible for unscrupulous therapists intentionally to take advantage of clients, but ethical therapists may unintentionally mistreat clients by leading them in directions that conform more to the therapist's perspective or bias than to perspectives that might be of greater help to the client.

Sigmund Freud (1856–1939), the father of psychoanalysis, asserted that there exists a psychological phenomenon known as *repression,* a mental defense mechanism by which we subconsciously suppress memories too painful or terrifying for us to deal with. Later in life these memories may resurface, having been buried in the subconscious for years or even decades. Although there is little laboratory evidence to support the concept of repression, therapists have received countless reports by clients who claim to have recovered memories of trauma, including stories by soldiers, refugees, and accident victims. Many of these recovered memories, upon further investigation, appear to be confirmed.

Reports of repressed memories of sexual abuse during childhood are particularly common. Some research indicates that as many as one in three women and one in six men will have been sexually abused in some way before they reach the age of 18. In the past decade, however, a controversy has arisen about the validity of many of the reports of repressed memories. A leading figure in this controversy is Dr. Elizabeth Loftus of the University of Washington, Seattle. In January 1994 Dr. Loftus and her associate Maryanne Garry published an article entitled "Repressed Memories of Childhood Trauma: Could Some of Them Be Suggested?" in *USA Today*. Loftus and Garry argue that some therapists, overly eager to help their clients find the root of their emotional problems, may suggest too forcefully the presence of repressed memories of sexual abuse. Clients eager to find any breakthrough to healing may then unknowingly invent memories of events that never happened. The *USA Today* article tells the following story:

> Gloria Grady is the child of devil-worshippers. Around an altar in their home, her family would don black robes and perform satanic rituals led by her father, a Baptist minister. Grady's father raped her repeatedly from the time she was 10 until she was in college, and her mother, brother, and grandfather sexually abused her. She was a "breeder" for the cult, providing them with aborted fetuses, and even an incestuous child when she was 14. The child was tossed into a fire as a sacrificial devil-offering. Now in her 30s, Grady has vivid memories of these childhood events, but, as reported in *D Magazine* (October 1991), there is no evidence that any of these memories are true.
>
> Grady didn't have these memories until she was about 27, shortly after she began "Christian counseling" at a Dallas-area clinic to grapple with what had been a lifelong weight problem. After an intensive hospitalization, she continued with weekly individual and group counseling. At first, her therapist suggested that she write down all the bad things that had happened in her life. A friend says Grady's list originally had rather benign entries, like the time her parents refused to let her square dance as a first-grader. Eventually, however, Grady came to remember incidents that were far worse. She began to have horrifying flashbacks, claiming that her father sexually abused her. With ensuing therapy sessions, she remembered more of these previously "repressed" memories, transforming her model Baptist family into a cult of childeating satanic ritualistic monsters. Her accusations left virtually no one in her family unaccused except a favorite aunt.
>
> Grady's parents denied all the allegations. Their attempts to intervene directly were unsuccessful, so they enlisted the aunt's help. When the group attempted to visit Grady at a halfway house, an altercation ensued and the police eventually ordered the relatives to leave. Shortly afterwards, the District Attorney's office served the family with papers requesting a protective order to prohibit any contact with Grady.

At the hearing, Grady's charges were refuted by other evidence. Her gynecological records revealed no indication of any sexual activity, let alone abortion or childbirth, during the period of alleged systematic rape. Grady remembered her mother hitting her so hard that she broke her collarbone; her orthopedic records showed the break to be the result of a spill in her walker as a 9-month-old child. Finally, photographs of Grady taken a few days before she supposedly gave birth showed that, although overweight, she most certainly was not pregnant.

Her therapist never testified, because of what Grady said was a joint agreement to end the relationship just prior to trial. Ultimately, the protective order request was turned down for lack of evidence, but Grady and her parents have not seen each other since. Most important, there still is no evidence that her memories are real. As a result of this and other reports of repressed memories that were later invalidated, substantial research is now being conducted concerning memories and repression.

12.2 Assignment: Analysis of an Ethical Problem

Many other ethical issues of interest to students of psychology, from the proper treatment of research subjects to the conduct of relationships among professionals, arise in relation to the professional duties of psychologists. The APA has studied many of these issues intensively, and the result of their efforts is a publication entitled the *Ethical Principles of Psychologists and Code of Conduct*, American Psychological Association (1992), commonly called the APA Ethics Code. To help you with the chapter's writing assignment, the Ethics Code is reprinted below, in its entirety.

Your assignment is to analyze an ethical issue that arises from a situation in which professional psychologists often find themselves. You will undertake this assignment by completing the following six tasks:

1. Situation selection
2. Issue(s) identification
3. Code section(s) identification
4. Code section(s) exposition
5. Issue resolution
6. Code critique

Write your paper in six sections that correspond to the above six tasks. Follow directions that appear in the paragraphs below for each section.

Situation Selection

Select a professional situation to analyze. You may select a situation from the following list of examples, identify an unlisted situation yourself, or write about a situation assigned by your instructor. *It is always a good idea to ask your instructor to approve the situation you have selected.* The following situations, all of which have occurred and continue to occur in real life, are merely examples of situations that you may want to consider. Remember, select *only one* situation unless directed otherwise by the instructor.

- A female client asks her male therapist to drive her home after a therapy session.
- Your research questionnaire includes the following item:
  I ☐ have ☐ have not been sexually abused.
- Although you (a research assistant) have written most of an article, your professor, who directed the project, expects to have her name listed first when the article is published.
- You are head of psychological services at the hospital. You ask your secretary to make coffee.
- A client admits to you that he hates his uncle and plans to kill him.
- Finding that some of the survey respondents did not complete your questionnaire, you fill in the absent data.
- As payment for your therapy services you accept three bushels of apples.
- Your advertisement in the yellow pages of the phone book includes the statement: "Come to Dr. Smith for a sure cure!"
- *Immediately* after showing your research subjects videos containing violence, you send them home.
- Professor John Smith invites his student, Miss Jones, to a private party to which other students are not invited.
- An insurance company representative requires you to *fax* him confidential information about one of your clients.
- A colleague is having sex with one of his patients.

Issue(s) Identification

Once you have selected a situation, identify the potential ethical issues, questions, problems, or dilemmas inherent in the situation. Suppose, for example, that you select the following situation: "Your psychology professor is an excellent therapist and you need counseling." What problems might arise in this situation? Are dual relationships involved? Are dual relationships a problem? A good way to proceed in identifying issues is to read the entire APA Ethics Code (printed below) at this point. As you read, make notations about any entry that may be relevant to the issue you have selected.

Code Section(s) Identification

Once you have read the APA Ethics Code, you are almost done with this part of the assignment. Reading back through the code, identify the specific section or sections that, upon further reflection, you find relevant to the ethical questions you have defined.

Code Section(s) Exposition

In a paragraph or two for each section, explain why the sections of the APA Ethics Code that you have selected are relevant to the situation you are analyzing.

Issue Resolution

Resolve the selected issue by applying to it the principles of the APA Ethics Code. If your selected situation is "Your psychology professor is an excellent therapist and you need counseling," for example, explain (1) what decision you should make with respect to asking your professor for therapy, (2) what sections of the APA Ethics Code led you to make this decision, and (3) why you interpreted those sections as leading to the decision you have made in this particular case.

Code Critique

Critique the APA Ethics Code for its strengths and weaknesses with respect to the method you have chosen for dealing with the situation you have selected. Does the code provide sufficient guidance for making a decision in your particular situation? Is the code too directive? Should the code be made more specific? Less specific? Taken as a whole, with its general principles and specific mandates and prohibitions, how well does the code fulfill its purpose, which is to provide ethical guidance for professional psychologists?

Your paper will be from five to ten pages in length and will follow all page format instructions indicated in Chapter 3 of this manual. It will consist of a cover sheet and the body of the paper. A reference page and appendices will not be necessary unless sources in addition to the APA Ethics Code are utilized.

12.3 The APA Code of Ethics

AMERICAN PSYCHOLOGICAL
ASSOCIATION

ETHICAL PRINCIPLES OF PSYCHOLOGISTS
AND CODE OF CONDUCT

TABLE of CONTENTS

8. RESOLVING ETHICAL ISSUES

INTRODUCTION

The American Psychological Association's (APA's) Ethical Principles of Psychologists and Code of Conduct (hereinafter referred to as the Ethics Code) consists of an Introduction, a Preamble, six General Principles (A–F), and specific Ethical Standards. The Introduction discusses the intent, organization, procedural considerations, and scope of application of the Ethics Code. The Preamble and General Principles are *aspirational* goals to guide psychologists toward the highest ideals of psychology. Although the Preamble and General Principles are not themselves enforceable rules, they should be considered by psychologists in arriving at an ethical course of action and may be considered by ethics bodies in interpreting the Ethical Standards. The Ethical Standards set forth *enforceable* rules for conduct as psychologists. Most of the Ethical Standards are written broadly, in order to apply to psychologists in varied roles, although the application of an Ethical Standard may vary depending on the context. The Ethical Standards are not exhaustive. The fact that a given conduct is not specifically addressed by the Ethics Code does not mean that it is necessarily either ethical or unethical.

Membership in the APA commits members to adhere to the APA Ethics Code and to the rules and procedures used to implement it. Psychologists and students, whether or not they are APA members, should be aware that the Ethics Code may be applied to them by state psychology boards, courts, or other public bodies.

This Ethics Code applies only to psychologists' work-related activities, that is, activities that are part of the psychologists' scientific and professional functions or that are psychological in nature. It includes the clinical or counseling practice of psychology, research, teaching, supervision of trainees, development of assessment instruments, conducting assessments, educational counseling, organizational consulting, social intervention, administration, and other activities as well. These work-related activities can be distinguished from the purely private conduct of a psychologist, which ordinarily is not within the purview of the Ethics Code.

The Ethics Code is intended to provide standards of professional conduct that can be applied by the APA and by other bodies that choose to adopt them. Whether or not a psychologist has violated the Ethics Code does not by itself determine whether he or she is legally liable in a court action, whether a contract is enforceable, or whether other legal consequences occur. These results are based on legal rather than ethical rules. However, compliance with or violation of the Ethics Code may be admissible as evidence in some legal proceedings, depending on the circumstances.

In the process of making decisions regarding their professional behavior, psychologists must consider this Ethics Code, in addition to applicable laws and psychology board regulations. If the Ethics Code establishes a higher standard of conduct than is required by law, psychologists must meet the higher ethical standard. If the Ethics Code standard appears to conflict with the requirements of law, then psychologists make known their commitment to the Ethics Code and take steps to resolve the conflict in a responsible manner. If neither law nor the Ethics Code resolves an issue, psychologists should consider other professional materials and the dictates of their own conscience, as well as seek consultation with others within the field when this is practical.

The procedures for filing, investigating, and resolving complaints of unethical conduct are described in the current Rules and Procedures of the APA Ethics Committee. The actions that APA may take for violations of the Ethics Code include actions such as reprimand, censure, termination of APA membership, and referral of the matter to other bodies. Complainants who seek remedies such as monetary damages in alleging ethical violations by a psychologist must resort to private negotiation, administrative bodies, or the courts. Actions that violate the Ethics Code may lead to the imposition of sanctions on a psychologist by bodies other than APA, including state psychological associations, other professional groups, psychology boards, other state or federal agencies, and payors for health services. In addition to actions for violation of the Ethics Code, the APA Bylaws provide that APA may take action against a member after his or her conviction of a felony, expulsion or suspension from an affiliated state psychological association, or suspension or loss of licensure.

PREAMBLE

Psychologists work to develop a valid and reliable body of scientific knowledge based on research. They may apply that knowledge to human behavior in a variety of contexts. In doing so, they perform many roles, such as researcher, educator, diagnostician, therapist, supervisor, consultant, administrator, social interventionist, and expert witness. Their goal is to broaden knowledge of behavior and, where appropriate, to apply it pragmatically to improve the condition of both the individual and society. Psychologists respect the central importance of freedom of inquiry and expression in research, teaching, and publication. They also strive to help the public in developing informed judgments and choices concerning human behavior. This Ethics Code provides a common set of values upon which psychologists build their professional and scientific work.

This Code is intended to provide both the general principles and the decision rules to cover most situations encountered by psychologists. It has as its primary goal the welfare and protection of the individuals and groups with whom psychologists work. It is the individual responsibility of each psychologist to aspire to the highest possible standards of conduct. Psychologists respect and protect human and civil rights, and do not knowingly participate in or condone unfair discriminatory practices.

The development of a dynamic set of ethical standards for a psychologist's work-related conduct requires a personal commitment to a lifelong effort to act ethically; to encourage ethical behavior by students, supervisees, employees, and colleagues, as appropriate; and to consult with others, as needed, concerning ethical problems. Each psychologist supplements, but does not violate, the Ethics Code's values and rules on the basis of guidance drawn from personal values, culture, and experience.

GENERAL PRINCIPLES

PRINCIPLE A: COMPETENCE

Psychologists strive to maintain high standards of competence in their work. They recognize the boundaries of their particular competencies and the limitations of their expertise. They provide only those services and use only those techniques for which they are qualified by education, training, or experience. Psychologists are cognizant of the fact that the competencies required in serving, teaching, and/or studying groups of people vary with the distinctive characteristics of those groups. In those areas in which recognized professional standards do not yet exist, psychologists exercise careful judgment and take appropriate precautions to protect the welfare of those with whom they work. They maintain knowledge of relevant scientific and professional information related to the services they render, and they recognize the need for ongoing education. Psychologists make appropriate use of scientific, professional, technical, and administrative resources.

PRINCIPLE B: INTEGRITY

Psychologists seek to promote integrity in the science, teaching, and practice of psychology. In these activities psychologists are honest, fair, and respectful of others. In describing or reporting their qualifications, services, products, fees, research, or teaching, they do not make statements that are false, misleading, or deceptive. Psychologists strive to be aware of their own belief systems, values, needs, and limitations and the effect of these on their work. To the extent feasible, they attempt to clarify for relevant parties the roles they are performing and to function appropriately in accordance with those roles. Psychologists avoid improper and potentially harmful dual relationships.

PRINCIPLE C: PROFESSIONAL AND SCIENTIFIC RESPONSIBILITY

Psychologists uphold professional standards of conduct, clarify their professional roles and obligations, accept appropriate responsibility for their behavior, and adapt their methods to the needs of different populations. Psychologists consult with, refer to, or cooperate with other professionals and institutions to the extent needed to serve the best interests of their patients, clients, or other recipients of their services. Psychologists' moral standards and conduct are personal matters to the same degree as is true for any other person, except as psychologists' conduct may compromise their professional responsibilities or reduce the public's trust in psychology and psychologists. Psychologists are concerned about the ethical compliance of their colleagues' scientific and professional conduct. When appropriate, they consult with colleagues in order to prevent or avoid unethical conduct.

PRINCIPLE D: RESPECT FOR PEOPLE'S RIGHTS AND DIGNITY

Psychologists accord appropriate respect to the fundamental rights, dignity, and worth of all people. They respect the rights of individuals to privacy, confidentiality, self-determination, and autonomy, mindful that legal and other obligations may lead to inconsistency and conflict with the exercise of these rights. Psychologists are aware of cultural, individual, and role differences, including those due to age, gender, race, ethnicity, national origin, religion, sexual orientation, disability, language, and socioeconomic status. Psychologists try to eliminate the effect on their work of biases based on those factors, and they do not knowingly participate in or condone unfair discriminatory practices.

PRINCIPLE E: CONCERN FOR OTHERS' WELFARE

Psychologists seek to contribute to the welfare of those with whom they interact professionally. In their professional actions, psychologists weigh the welfare and rights of their patients or clients, students, supervisees, human research participants, and other affected persons, and the welfare of animal subjects of research. When conflicts occur among psychologists' obligations or concerns, they attempt to resolve these conflicts and to perform their roles in a responsible fashion that avoids or minimizes harm. Psychologists are sensitive to real and ascribed differences in power between themselves and others, and they do not exploit or mislead other people during or after professional relationships.

PRINCIPLE F: SOCIAL RESPONSIBILITY

Psychologists are aware of their professional and scientific responsibilities to the community and the society in which they work and live. They apply and make public their knowledge of psychology in order to contribute to human welfare. Psychologists are concerned about and work to mitigate the causes of human suffering. When undertaking research, they strive to advance human welfare and the science of psychology. Psychologists try to avoid misuse of their work. Psychologists comply with the law and encourage the development of law and social policy that serve the interests of their patients and clients and the public. They are encouraged to contribute a portion of their professional time for little or no personal advantage.

ETHICAL STANDARDS

1. GENERAL STANDARDS

These General Standards are potentially applicable to the professional and scientific activities of all psychologists.

1.01 Applicability of the Ethics Code.
The activity of a psychologist subject to the Ethics Code may be reviewed under these Ethical Standards only if the activity is part of his or her work-related functions or the activity is psychological in nature. Personal activities having no connection to or effect on psychological roles are not subject to the Ethics Code.

1.02 Relationship of Ethics and Law.
If psychologists' ethical responsibilities conflict with law, psychologists make known their commitment to the Ethics Code and take steps to resolve the conflict in a responsible manner.

1.03 Professional and Scientific Relationship.
Psychologists provide diagnostic, therapeutic, teaching, research, supervisory, consultative, or other psychological services only in the context of a defined professional or scientific relationship or role. (See also Standards 2.01, Evaluation, Diagnosis, and Interventions in Professional Context, and 7.02, Forensic Assessments.)

1.04 Boundaries of Competence.
(a) Psychologists provide services, teach, and conduct research only within the boundaries of their competence, based on their education, training, supervised experience, or appropriate professional experience.
(b) Psychologists provide services, teach, or conduct research in new areas or involving new techniques only after first undertaking appropriate study, training, supervision, and/or consultation from persons who are competent in those areas or techniques.
(c) In those emerging areas in which generally recognized standards for preparatory training do not yet exist, psychologists nevertheless take reasonable steps to ensure the competence of their work and to protect patients, clients, students, research participants, and others from harm.

1.05 Maintaining Expertise.
Psychologists who engage in assessment, therapy, teaching, research, organizational consulting, or other professional activities maintain a reasonable level of awareness of current scientific and professional information in their fields of activity, and undertake ongoing efforts to maintain competence in the skills they use.

1.06 Basis for Scientific and Professional Judgments.
Psychologists rely on scientifically and professionally derived knowledge when making scientific or professional judgments or when engaging in scholarly or professional endeavors.

1.07 Describing the Nature and Results of Psychological Services.
(a) When psychologists provide assessment, evaluation, treatment, counseling, supervision, teaching, consultation, research, or other psychological services to an individual, a group, or an organization, they provide, using language that is reasonably understandable to the recipient of those services, appropriate information beforehand about the nature of such services and appropriate information later about results and conclusions. (See also Standard 2.09, Explaining Assessment Results.)
(b) If psychologists will be precluded by law or by organizational roles from providing such information to particular individuals or groups, they so inform those individuals or groups at the outset of the service.

1.08 Human Differences.
Where differences of age, gender, race, ethnicity, national origin, religion, sexual orientation, disability, language, or socioeconomic status significantly affect psychologists' work concerning particular individuals or groups, psychologists obtain the training, experience, consultation, or supervision necessary to ensure the competence of their services, or they make appropriate referrals.

1.09 Respecting Others.
In their work-related activities, psychologists respect the rights of others to hold values, attitudes, and opinions that differ from their own.

1.10 Nondiscrimination.
In their work-related activities, psychologists do not engage in unfair discrimination based on age, gender, race, ethnicity, national origin, religion, sexual orientation, disability, socioeconomic status, or any basis proscribed by law.

1.11 Sexual Harassment.
(a) Psychologists do not engage in sexual harassment. Sexual harassment is sexual solicitation, physical advances, or verbal or nonverbal conduct that is sexual in nature, that occurs in connection with the psychologist's activities or roles as a psychologist, and that either: (1) is unwelcome, is offensive, or creates a hostile workplace environment, and the psychologist knows or is told this; or (2) is sufficiently severe or intense to be abusive to a reasonable person in the context. Sexual harassment can consist of a single intense or severe act or of multiple persistent or pervasive acts.

(b) Psychologists accord sexual-harassment complainants and respondents dignity and respect. Psychologists do not participate in denying a person academic admittance or advancement, employment, tenure, or promotion, based solely upon their having made, or their being the subject of, sexual harassment charges. This does not preclude taking action based upon the outcome of such proceedings or consideration of other appropriate information.

1.12 Other Harassment.
Psychologists do not knowingly engage in behavior that is harassing or demeaning to persons with whom they interact in their work based on factors such as those persons' age, gender, race, ethnicity, national origin, religion, sexual orientation, disability, language, or socioeconomic status.

1.13 Personal Problems and Conflicts.
(a) Psychologists recognize that their personal problems and conflicts may interfere with their effectiveness. Accordingly, they refrain from undertaking an activity when they know or should know that their personal problems are likely to lead to harm to a patient, client, colleague, student, research participant, or other person to whom they may owe a professional or scientific obligation.
(b) In addition, psychologists have an obligation to be alert to signs of, and to obtain assistance for, their personal problems at an early stage, in order to prevent significantly impaired performance.
(c) When psychologists become aware of personal problems that may interfere with their performing work-related duties adequately, they take appropriate measures, such as obtaining professional consultation or assistance, and determine whether they should limit, suspend, or terminate their work-related duties.

1.14 Avoiding Harm.
Psychologists take reasonable steps to avoid harming their patients or clients, research participants, students, and others with whom they work, and to minimize harm where it is foreseeable and unavoidable.

1.15 Misuse of Psychologists' Influence.
Because psychologists' scientific and professional judgments and actions may affect the lives of others, they are alert to and guard against personal, financial, social, organizational, or political factors that might lead to misuse of their influence.

1.16 Misuse of Psychologists' Work.
(a) Psychologists do not participate in activities in which it appears likely that their skills or data will be misused by others, unless corrective mechanisms are available. (See also Standard 7.04, Truthfulness and Candor.)
(b) If psychologists learn of misuse or misrepresentation of their work, they take reasonable steps to correct or minimize the misuse or misrepresentation.

1.17 Multiple Relationships.
(a) In many communities and situations, it may not be feasible or reasonable for psychologists to avoid social or other nonprofessional contacts with per-

sons such as patients, clients, students, supervisees, or research participants. Psychologists must always be sensitive to the potential harmful effects of other contacts on their work and on those persons with whom they deal. A psychologist refrains from entering into or promising another personal, scientific, professional, financial, or other relationship with such persons if it appears likely that such a relationship reasonably might impair the psychologist's objectivity or otherwise interfere with the psychologist's effectively performing his or her functions as a psychologist, or might harm or exploit the other party.

(b) Likewise, whenever feasible, a psychologist refrains from taking on professional or scientific obligations when pre-existing relationships would create a risk of such harm.

(c) If a psychologist finds that, due to unforeseen factors, a potentially harmful multiple relationship has arisen, the psychologist attempts to resolve it with due regard for the best interests of the affected person and maximal compliance with the Ethics Code.

1.18 Barter (With Patients or Clients).
Psychologists ordinarily refrain from accepting goods, services, or other non-monetary remuneration from patients or clients in return for psychological services because such arrangements create inherent potential for conflicts, exploitation, and distortion of the professional relationship. A psychologist may participate in bartering only if (1) it is not clinically contraindicated, and (2) the relationship is not exploitative. (See also Standards 1.17, Multiple Relationships, and 1.25, Fees and Financial Arrangements.)

1.19 Exploitative Relationships.
(a) Psychologists do not exploit persons over whom they have supervisory, evaluative, or other authority such as students, supervisees, employees, research participants, and clients or patients. (See also Standards 4.05–4.07 regarding sexual involvement with clients or patients.)

(b) Psychologists do not engage in sexual relationships with students or supervisees in training over whom the psychologist has evaluative or direct authority, because such relationships are so likely to impair judgment or be exploitative.

1.20 Consultations and Referrals.
(a) Psychologists arrange for appropriate consultations and referrals based principally on the best interests of their patients or clients, with appropriate consent, and subject to other relevant considerations, including applicable law and contractual obligations. (See also Standards 5.01, Discussing the Limits of Confidentiality, and 5.06, Consultations.)

(b) When indicated and professionally appropriate, psychologists cooperate with other professionals in order to serve their patients or clients effectively and appropriately.

(c) Psychologists' referral practices are consistent with law.

1.21 Third-Party Requests for Services.
(a) When a psychologist agrees to provide services to a person or entity at the request of a third party, the psychologist clarifies to the extent feasible, at the

outset of the service, the nature of the relationship with each party. This clarification includes the role of the psychologist (such as therapist, organizational consultant, diagnostician, or expert witness), the probable uses of the services provided or the information obtained, and the fact that there may be limits to confidentiality.

(b) If there is a foreseeable risk of the psychologist's being called upon to perform conflicting roles because of the involvement of a third party, the psychologist clarifies the nature and direction of his or her responsibilities, keeps all parties appropriately informed as matters develop, and resolves the situation in accordance with this Ethics Code.

1.22 Delegation to and Supervision of Subordinates.
(a) Psychologists delegate to their employees, supervisees, and research assistants only those responsibilities that such persons can reasonably be expected to perform competently, on the basis of their education, training, or experience, either independently or with the level of supervision being provided.
(b) Psychologists provide proper training and supervision to their employees or supervisees and take reasonable steps to see that such persons perform services responsibly, competently, and ethically.
(c) If institutional policies, procedures, or practices prevent fulfillment of this obligation, psychologists attempt to modify their role or to correct the situation to the extent feasible.

1.23 Documentation of Professional and Scientific Work.
(a) Psychologists appropriately document their professional and scientific work in order to facilitate provision of services later by them or by other professionals, to ensure accountability, and to meet other requirements of institutions or the law.
(b) When psychologists have reason to believe that records of their professional services will be used in legal proceedings involving recipients of or participants in their work, they have a responsibility to create and maintain documentation in the kind of detail and quality that would be consistent with reasonable scrutiny in an adjudicative forum. (See also Standard 7.01, Professionalism, under Forensic Activities.)

1.24 Records and Data.
Psychologists create, maintain, disseminate, store, retain, and dispose of records and data relating to their research, practice, and other work in accordance with law and in a manner that permits compliance with the requirements of this Ethics Code. (See also Standard 5.04, Maintenance of Records.)

1.25 Fees and Financial Arrangements.
(a) As early as is feasible in a professional or scientific relationship, the psychologist and the patient, client, or other appropriate recipient of psychological services reach an agreement specifying the compensation and the billing arrangements.

(b) Psychologists do not exploit recipients of services or payors with respect to fees.

(c) Psychologists' fee practices are consistent with law.

(d) Psychologists do not misrepresent their fees.

(e) If limitations to services can be anticipated because of limitations in financing, this is discussed with the patient, client, or other appropriate recipient of services as early as is feasible. (See also Standard 4.08, Interruption of Services.)

(f) If the patient, client, or other recipient of services does not pay for services as agreed, and if the psychologist wishes to use collection agencies or legal measures to collect the fees, the psychologist first informs the person that such measures will be taken and provides that person an opportunity to make prompt payment. (See also Standard 5.11, Withholding Records for Nonpayment.)

1.26 Accuracy in Reports to Payors and Funding Sources.
In their reports to payors for services or sources of research funding, psychologists accurately state the nature of the research or service provided, the fees or charges, and where applicable, the identity of the provider, the findings, and the diagnosis. (See also Standard 5.05, Disclosures.)

1.27 Referrals and Fees.
When a psychologist pays, receives payment from, or divides fees with another professional other than in an employer-employee relationship, the payment to each is based on the services (clinical, consultative, administrative, or other) provided and is not based on the referral itself.

2. EVALUATION, ASSESSMENT, OR INTERVENTION

2.01 Evaluation, Diagnosis, and Interventions in Professional Context.
(a) Psychologists perform evaluations, diagnostic services, or interventions only within the context of a defined professional relationship. (See also Standards 1.03, Professional and Scientific Relationship.)

(b) Psychologists' assessments, recommendations, reports, and psychological diagnostic or evaluative statements are based on information and techniques (including personal interviews of the individual when appropriate) sufficient to provide appropriate substantiation for their findings. (See also Standard 7.02, Forensic Assessments.)

2.02 Competence and Appropriate Use of Assessments and Interventions.
(a) Psychologists who develop, administer, score, interpret, or use psychological assessment techniques, interviews, tests, or instruments do so in a manner and for purposes that are appropriate in light of the research on or evidence of the usefulness and proper application of the techniques.

(b) Psychologists refrain from misuse of assessment techniques, interventions, results, and interpretations and take reasonable steps to prevent others from misusing the information these techniques provide. This includes refraining from releasing raw test results or raw data to persons, other than to patients or clients as appropriate, who are not qualified to use such information. (See also Standards 1.02, Relationship of Ethics and Law, and 1.04, Boundaries of Competence.)

2.03 Test Construction.
Psychologists who develop and conduct research with tests and other assessment techniques use scientific procedures and current professional knowledge for test design, standardization, validation, reduction or elimination of bias, and recommendations for use.

2.04 Use of Assessment in General and With Special Populations.
(a) Psychologists who perform interventions or administer, score, interpret, or use assessment techniques are familiar with the reliability, validation, and related standardization or outcome studies of, and proper applications and uses of, the techniques they use.
(b) Psychologists recognize limits to the certainty with which diagnoses, judgments, or predictions can be made about individuals.
(c) Psychologists attempt to identify situations in which particular interventions or assessment techniques or norms may not be applicable or may require adjustment in administration or interpretation because of factors such as individuals' gender, age, race, ethnicity, national origin, religion, sexual orientation, disability, language, or socioeconomic status.

2.05 Interpreting Assessment Results.
When interpreting assessment results, including automated interpretations, psychologists take into account the various test factors and characteristics of the person being assessed that might affect psychologists' judgments or reduce the accuracy of their interpretations. They indicate any significant reservations they have about the accuracy or limitations of their interpretations.

2.06 Unqualified Persons.
Psychologists do not promote the use of psychological assessment techniques by unqualified persons. (See also Standard 1.22, Delegation to and Supervision of Subordinates.)

2.07 Obsolete Tests and Outdated Test Results.
(a) Psychologists do not base their assessment or intervention decisions or recommendations on data or test results that are outdated for the current purpose.
(b) Similarly, psychologists do not base such decisions or recommendations on tests and measures that are obsolete and not useful for the current purpose.

2.08 Test Scoring and Interpretation Services.
(a) Psychologists who offer assessment or scoring procedures to other professionals accurately describe the purpose, norms, validity, reliability, and applications of the procedures and any special qualifications applicable to their use.
(b) Psychologists select scoring and interpretation services (including automated services) on the basis of evidence of the validity of the program and procedures as well as on other appropriate considerations.

(c) Psychologists retain appropriate responsibility for the appropriate application, interpretation, and use of assessment instruments, whether they score and interpret such tests themselves or use automated or other services.

2.09 Explaining Assessment Results.
Unless the nature of the relationship is clearly explained to the person being assessed in advance and precludes provision of an explanation of results (such as in some organizational consulting, pre-employment or security screenings, and forensic evaluations), psychologists ensure that an explanation of the results is provided using language that is reasonably understandable to the person assessed or to another legally authorized person on behalf of the client. Regardless of whether the scoring and interpretation are done by the psychologist, by assistants, or by automated or other outside services, psychologists take reasonable steps to ensure that appropriate explanations of results are given.

2.10 Maintaining Test Security.
Psychologists make reasonable efforts to maintain the integrity and security of tests and other assessment techniques consistent with law, contractual obligations, and in a manner that permits compliance with the requirements of this Ethics Code. (See also Standard 1.02, Relationship of Ethics and Law.)

3. ADVERTISING AND OTHER PUBLIC STATEMENTS

3.01 Definition of Public Statements.
Psychologists comply with this Ethics Code in public statements relating to their professional services, products, or publications or to the field of psychology. Public statements include but are not limited to paid or unpaid advertising, brochures, printed matter, directory listings, personal resumes or curriculum vitae, interviews or comments for use in media, statements in legal proceedings, lectures and public oral presentations, and published materials.

3.02 Statements by Others.
(a) Psychologists who engage others to create or place public statements that promote their professional practice, products, or activities retain professional responsibility for such statements.
(b) In addition, psychologists make reasonable efforts to prevent others whom they do not control (such as employers, publishers, sponsors, organizational clients, and representatives of the print or broadcast media) from making deceptive statements concerning psychologists' practice or professional or scientific activities.
(c) If psychologists learn of deceptive statements about their work made by others, psychologists make reasonable efforts to correct such statements.
(d) Psychologists do not compensate employees of press, radio, television, or other communication media in return for publicity in a news item.
(e) A paid advertisement relating to the psychologist's activities must be identified as such, unless it is already apparent from the context.

3.03 Avoidance of False or Deceptive Statements.
(a) Psychologists do not make public statements that are false, deceptive, misleading, or fraudulent, either because of what they state, convey, or suggest or because of what they omit, concerning their research, practice, or other work activities or those of persons or organizations with which they are affiliated. As examples (and not in limitation) of this standard, psychologists do not make false or deceptive statements concerning (1) their training, experience, or competence; (2) their academic degrees; (3) their credentials; (4) their institutional or association affiliations; (5) their services; (6) the scientific or clinical basis for, or results or degree of success of, their services; (7) their fees; or (8) their publications or research findings. (See also Standards 6.15, Deception in Research, and 6.18, Providing Participants With Information About the Study.)
(b) Psychologists claim as credentials for their psychological work, only degrees that (1) were earned from a regionally accredited educational institution or (2) were the basis for psychology licensure by the state in which they practice.

3.04 Media Presentations.
When psychologists provide advice or comment by means of public lectures, demonstrations, radio or television programs, prerecorded tapes, printed articles, mailed material, or other media, they take reasonable precautions to ensure that (1) the statements are based on appropriate psychological literature and practice, (2) the statements are otherwise consistent with this Ethics Code, and (3) the recipients of the information are not encouraged to infer that a relationship has been established with them personally.

3.05 Testimonials.
Psychologists do not solicit testimonials from current psychotherapy clients or patients or other persons who because of their particular circumstances are vulnerable to undue influence.

3.06 In-Person Solicitation.
Psychologists do not engage, directly or through agents, in uninvited in-person solicitation of business from actual or potential psychotherapy patients or clients or other persons who because of their particular circumstances are vulnerable to undue influence. However, this does not preclude attempting to implement appropriate collateral contacts with significant others for the purpose of benefiting an already engaged therapy patient.

4. THERAPY

4.01 Structuring the Relationship.
(a) Psychologists discuss with clients or patients as early as is feasible in the therapeutic relationship appropriate issues, such as the nature and anticipated course of therapy, fees, and confidentiality. (See also Standards 1.25,

Fees and Financial Arrangements, and 5.01, Discussing the Limits of Confidentiality.)

(b) When the psychologist's work with clients or patients will be supervised, the above discussion includes that fact, and the name of the supervisor, when the supervisor has legal responsibility for the case.

(c) When the therapist is a student intern, the client or patient is informed of that fact.

(d) Psychologists make reasonable efforts to answer patients' questions and to avoid apparent misunderstandings about therapy. Whenever possible, psychologists provide oral and/or written information, using language that is reasonably understandable to the patient or client.

4.02 Informed Consent to Therapy.

(a) Psychologists obtain appropriate informed consent to therapy or related procedures, using language that is reasonably understandable to participants. The content of informed consent will vary depending on many circumstances; however, informed consent generally implies that the person (1) has the capacity to consent, (2) has been informed of significant information concerning the procedure, (3) has freely and without undue influence expressed consent, and (4) consent has been appropriately documented.

(b) When persons are legally incapable of giving informed consent, psychologists obtain informed permission from a legally authorized person, if such substitute consent is permitted by law.

(c) In addition, psychologists (1) inform those persons who are legally incapable of giving informed consent about the proposed interventions in a manner commensurate with the persons' psychological capacities, (2) seek their assent to those interventions, and (3) consider such persons' preferences and best interests.

4.03 Couple and Family Relationships.

(a) When a psychologist agrees to provide services to several persons who have a relationship (such as husband and wife or parents and children), the psychologist attempts to clarify at the outset (1) which of the individuals are patients or clients and (2) the relationship the psychologist will have with each person. This clarification includes the role of the psychologist and the probable uses of the services provided or the information obtained. (See also Standard 5.01, Discussing the Limits of Confidentiality.)

(b) As soon as it becomes apparent that the psychologist may be called on to perform potentially conflicting roles (such as marital counselor to husband and wife, and then witness for one party in a divorce proceeding), the psychologist attempts to clarify and adjust, or withdraw from, roles appropriately. (See also Standard 7.03, Clarification of Role, under Forensic Activities.)

4.04 Providing Mental Health Services to Those Served by Others.

In deciding whether to offer or provide services to those already receiving mental health services elsewhere, psychologists carefully consider the treatment issues and the potential patient's or client's welfare. The psychologist discusses these issues with the patient or client, or another legally authorized person on behalf of the client, in order to minimize the risk of confusion and conflict, consults with the other service providers when appropriate, and proceeds with caution and sensitivity to the therapeutic issues.

4.05 Sexual Intimacies With Current Patients or Clients.
Psychologists do not engage in sexual intimacies with current patients or clients.

4.06 Therapy With Former Sexual Partners.
Psychologists do not accept as therapy patients or clients persons with whom they have engaged in sexual intimacies.

4.07 Sexual Intimacies With Former Therapy Patients.
(a) Psychologists do not engage in sexual intimacies with a former therapy patient or client for at least two years after cessation or termination of professional services.
(b) Because sexual intimacies with a former therapy patient or client are so frequently harmful to the patient or client, and because such intimacies undermine public confidence in the psychology profession and thereby deter the public's use of needed services, psychologists do not engage in sexual intimacies with former therapy patients and clients even after a two-year interval except in the most unusual circumstances. The psychologist who engages in such activity after the two years following cessation or termination of treatment bears the burden of demonstrating that there has been no exploitation, in light of all relevant factors, including (1) the amount of time that has passed since therapy terminated, (2) the nature and duration of the therapy, (3) the circumstances of termination, (4) the patient's or client's personal history, (5) the patient's or client's current mental status, (6) the likelihood of adverse impact on the patient or client and others, and (7) any statements or actions made by the therapist during the course of therapy suggesting or inviting the possibility of a post-termination sexual or romantic relationship with the patient or client. (See also Standard 1.17, Multiple Relationships.)

4.08 Interruption of Services.
(a) Psychologists make reasonable efforts to plan for facilitating care in the event that psychological services are interrupted by factors such as the psychologist's illness, death, unavailability, or relocation or by the client's relocation or financial limitations. (See also Standard 5.09, Preserving Records and Data.)
(b) When entering into employment or contractual relationships, psychologists provide for orderly and appropriate resolution of responsibility for patient or client care in the event that the employment or contractual relationship ends, with paramount consideration given to the welfare of the patient or client.

4.09 Terminating the Professional Relationship.

(a) Psychologists do not abandon patients or clients. (See also Standard 1.25e, under Fees and Financial Arrangements.)

(b) Psychologists terminate a professional relationship when it becomes reasonably clear that the patient or client no longer needs the service, is not benefiting, or is being harmed by continued service.

(c) Prior to termination for whatever reason, except where precluded by the patient's or client's conduct, the psychologist discusses the patient's or client's views and needs, provides appropriate pretermination counseling, suggests alternative service providers as appropriate, and takes other reasonable steps to facilitate transfer of responsibility to another provider if the patient or client needs one immediately.

5. PRIVACY AND CONFIDENTIALITY

These Standards are potentially applicable to the professional and scientific activities of all psychologists.

5.01 Discussing the Limits of Confidentiality.

(a) Psychologists discuss with persons and organizations with whom they establish a scientific or professional relationship (including, to the extent feasible, minors and their legal representatives) (1) the relevant limitations on confidentiality, including limitations where applicable in group, marital, and family therapy or in organizational consulting, and (2) the foreseeable uses of the information generated through their services.

(b) Unless it is not feasible or is contraindicated, the discussion of confidentiality occurs at the outset of the relationship and thereafter as new circumstances may warrant.

(c) Permission for electronic recording of interviews is secured from clients and patients.

5.02 Maintaining Confidentiality.

Psychologists have a primary obligation and take reasonable precautions to respect the confidentiality rights of those with whom they work or consult, recognizing that confidentiality may be established by law, institutional rules, or professional or scientific relationships. (See also Standard 6.26, Professional Reviewers.)

5.03 Minimizing Intrusions on Privacy.

(a) In order to minimize intrusions on privacy, psychologists include in written and oral reports, consultations, and the like, only information germane to the purpose for which the communication is made.

(b) Psychologists discuss confidential information obtained in clinical or consulting relationships, or evaluative data concerning patients, individual or organizational clients, students, research participants, supervisees, and employees, only for appropriate scientific or professional purposes and only with persons clearly concerned with such matters.

5.04 Maintenance of Records.
Psychologists maintain appropriate confidentiality in creating, storing, accessing, transferring, and disposing of records under their control, whether these are written, automated, or in any other medium. Psychologists maintain and dispose of records in accordance with law and in a manner that permits compliance with the requirements of this Ethics Code.

5.05 Disclosures.
(a) Psychologists disclose confidential information without the consent of the individual only as mandated by law, or where permitted by law for a valid purpose, such as (1) to provide needed professional services to the patient or the individual or organizational client, (2) to obtain appropriate professional consultations, (3) to protect the patient or client or others from harm, or (4) to obtain payment for services, in which instance disclosure is limited to the minimum that is necessary to achieve the purpose.
(b) Psychologists also may disclose confidential information with the appropriate consent of the patient or the individual or organizational client (or of another legally authorized person on behalf of the patient or client), unless prohibited by law.

5.06 Consultations.
When consulting with colleagues, (1) psychologists do not share confidential information that reasonably could lead to the identification of a patient, client, research participant, or other person or organization with whom they have a confidential relationship unless they have obtained the prior consent of the person or organization or the disclosure cannot be avoided, and (2) they share information only to the extent necessary to achieve the purposes of the consultation. (See also Standard 5.02, Maintaining Confidentiality.)

5.07 Confidential Information in Databases.
(a) If confidential information concerning recipients of psychological services is to be entered into databases or systems of records available to persons whose access has not been consented to by the recipient, then psychologists use coding or other techniques to avoid the inclusion of personal identifiers.
(b) If a research protocol approved by an institutional review board or similar body requires the inclusion of personal identifiers, such identifiers are deleted before the information is made accessible to persons other than those of whom the subject was advised.
(c) If such deletion is not feasible, then before psychologists transfer such data to others or review such data collected by others, they take reasonable steps to determine that appropriate consent of personally identifiable individuals has been obtained.

5.08 Use of Confidential Information for Didactic or Other Purposes.
(a) Psychologists do not disclose in their writings, lectures, or other public media, confidential, personally identifiable information concerning their patients, individual or organizational clients, students, research participants, or other recipients of their services that they obtained during the course of

their work, unless the person or organization has consented in writing or unless there is other ethical or legal authorization for doing so.

(b) Ordinarily, in such scientific and professional presentations, psychologists disguise confidential information concerning such persons or organizations so that they are not individually identifiable to others and so that discussions do not cause harm to subjects who might identify themselves.

5.09 Preserving Records and Data.

A psychologist makes plans in advance so that confidentiality of records and data is protected in the event of the psychologist's death, incapacity, or withdrawal from the position or practice.

5.10 Ownership of Records and Data.

Recognizing that ownership of records and data is governed by legal principles, psychologists take reasonable and lawful steps so that records and data remain available to the extent needed to serve the best interests of patients, individual or organizational clients, research participants, or appropriate others.

5.11 Withholding Records for Nonpayment.

Psychologists may not withhold records under their control that are requested and imminently needed for a patient's or client's treatment solely because payment has not been received, except as otherwise provided by law.

6. TEACHING, TRAINING SUPERVISION, RESEARCH, AND PUBLISHING

6.01 Design of Education and Training Programs.

Psychologists who are responsible for education and training programs seek to ensure that the programs are competently designed, provide the proper experiences, and meet the requirements for licensure, certification, or other goals for which claims are made by the program.

6.02 Descriptions of Education and Training Programs.

(a) Psychologists responsible for education and training programs seek to ensure that there is a current and accurate description of the program content, training goals and objectives, and requirements that must be met for satisfactory completion of the program. This information must be made readily available to all interested parties.

(b) Psychologists seek to ensure that statements concerning their course outlines are accurate and not misleading, particularly regarding the subject matter to be covered, bases for evaluating progress, and the nature of course experiences. (See also Standard 3.03, Avoidance of False or Deceptive Statements.)

(c) To the degree to which they exercise control, psychologists responsible for announcements, catalogs, brochures, or advertisements describing workshops, seminars, or other non-degree-granting educational programs ensure that they accurately describe the audience for which the program is intended, the educational objectives, the presenters, and the fees involved.

6.03 Accuracy and Objectivity in Teaching.
(a) When engaged in teaching or training, psychologists present psychological information accurately and with a reasonable degree of objectivity.
(b) When engaged in teaching or training, psychologists recognize the power they hold over students or supervisees and therefore make reasonable efforts to avoid engaging in conduct that is personally demeaning to students or supervisees. (See also Standards 1.09, Respecting Others, and 1.12, Other Harassment.)

6.04 Limitation on Teaching.
Psychologists do not teach the use of techniques or procedures that require specialized training, licensure, or expertise, including but not limited to hypnosis, biofeedback, and projective techniques, to individuals who lack the prerequisite training, legal scope of practice, or expertise.

6.05 Assessing Student and Supervisee Performance.
(a) In academic and supervisory relationships, psychologists establish an appropriate process for providing feedback to students and supervisees.
(b) Psychologists evaluate students and supervisees on the basis of their actual performance on relevant and established program requirements.

6.06 Planning Research.
(a) Psychologists design, conduct, and report research in accordance with recognized standards of scientific competence and ethical research.
(b) Psychologists plan their research so as to minimize the possibility that results will be misleading.
(c) In planning research, psychologists consider its ethical acceptability under the Ethics Code. If an ethical issue is unclear, psychologists seek to resolve the issue through consultation with institutional review boards, animal care and use committees, peer consultations, or other proper mechanisms.
(d) Psychologists take reasonable steps to implement appropriate protections for the rights and welfare of human participants, other persons affected by the research, and the welfare of animal subjects.

6.07 Responsibility.
(a) Psychologists conduct research competently and with due concern for the dignity and welfare of the participants.
(b) Psychologists are responsible for the ethical conduct of research conducted by them or by others under their supervision or control.
(c) Researchers and assistants are permitted to perform only those tasks for which they are appropriately trained and prepared.
(d) As part of the process of development and implementation of research projects, psychologists consult those with expertise concerning any special population under investigation or most likely to be affected.

6.08 Compliance With Law and Standards.
Psychologists plan and conduct research in a manner consistent with federal and state law and regulations, as well as professional standards governing the

conduct of research, and particularly those standards governing research with human participants and animal subjects.

6.09 Institutional Approval.
Psychologists obtain from host institutions or organizations appropriate approval prior to conducting research, and they provide accurate information about their research proposals. They conduct the research in accordance with the approved research protocol.

6.10 Research Responsibilities.
Prior to conducting research (except research involving only anonymous surveys, naturalistic observations, or similar research), psychologists enter into an agreement with participants that clarifies the nature of the research and the responsibilities of each party.

6.11 Informed Consent to Research.
(a) Psychologists use language that is reasonably understandable to research participants in obtaining their appropriate informed consent (except as provided in Standard 6.12, Dispensing With Informed Consent). Such informed consent is appropriately documented.
(b) Using language that is reasonably understandable to participants, psychologists inform participants of the nature of the research; they inform participants that they are free to participate or to decline to participate or to withdraw from the research; they explain the foreseeable consequences of declining or withdrawing; they inform participants of significant factors that may be expected to influence their willingness to participate (such as risks, discomfort, adverse effects, or limitations on confidentiality, except as provided in Standard 6.15, Deception in Research); and they explain other aspects about which the prospective participants inquire.
(c) When psychologists conduct research with individuals such as students or subordinates, psychologists take special care to protect the prospective participants from adverse consequences of declining or withdrawing from participation.
(d) When research participation is a course requirement or opportunity for extra credit, the prospective participant is given the choice of equitable alternative activities.
(e) For persons who are legally incapable of giving informed consent, psychologists nevertheless (1) provide an appropriate explanation, (2) obtain the participant's assent, and (3) obtain appropriate permission from a legally authorized person, if such substitute consent is permitted by law.

6.12 Dispensing With Informed Consent.
Before determining that planned research (such as research involving only anonymous questionnaires, naturalistic observations, or certain kinds of archival research) does not require the informed consent of research participants, psychologists consider applicable regulations and institutional review board requirements, and they consult with colleagues as appropriate.

6.13 Informed Consent in Research Filming or Recording.
Psychologists obtain informed consent from research participants prior to filming or recording them in any form, unless the research involves simply naturalistic observations in public places and it is not anticipated that the recording
will be used in a manner that could cause personal identification or harm.

6.14 Offering Inducements for Research Participants.
(a) In offering professional services as an inducement to obtain research participants, psychologists make clear the nature of the services, as well as the
risks, obligations, and limitations. (See also Standard 1.18, Barter [With Patients or Clients].)
(b) Psychologists do not offer excessive or inappropriate financial or other
inducements to obtain research participants, particularly when it might tend
to coerce participation.

6.15 Deception in Research.
(a) Psychologists do not conduct a study involving deception unless they
have determined that the use of deceptive techniques is justified by the
study's prospective scientific, educational, or applied value and that equally
effective alternative procedures that do not use deception are not feasible.
(b) Psychologists never deceive research participants about significant aspects that would affect their willingness to participate, such as physical risks,
discomfort, or unpleasant emotional experiences.
(c) Any other deception that is an integral feature of the design and conduct
of an experiment must be explained to participants as early as is feasible,
preferably at the conclusion of their participation, but no later than at the
conclusion of the research. (See also Standard 6.18, Providing Participants
With Information About the Study.)

6.16 Sharing and Utilizing Data.
Psychologists inform research participants of their anticipated sharing or further use of personally identifiable research data and of the possibility of
unanticipated future uses.

6.17 Minimizing Invasiveness.
In conducting research, psychologists interfere with the participants or mi-
lieu from which data are collected only in a manner that is warranted by an
appropriate research design and that is consistent with psychologists' roles as
scientific investigators.

6.18 Providing Participants With Information About the Study.
(a) Psychologists provide a prompt opportunity for participants to obtain appropriate information about the nature, results, and conclusions of the research, and psychologists attempt to correct any misconceptions that
participants may have.
(b) If scientific or humane values justify delaying or withholding this information, psychologists take reasonable measures to reduce the risk of harm.

6.19 Honoring Commitments.
Psychologists take reasonable measures to honor all commitments they have made to research participants.

6.20 Care and Use of Animals in Research.
(a) Psychologists who conduct research involving animals treat them humanely.
(b) Psychologists acquire, care for, use, and dispose of animals in compliance with current federal, state, and local laws and regulations, and with professional standards.
(c) Psychologists trained in research methods and experienced in the care of laboratory animals supervise all procedures involving animals and are responsible for ensuring appropriate consideration of their comfort, health, and humane treatment.
(d) Psychologists ensure that all individuals using animals under their supervision have received instruction in research methods and in the care, maintenance, and handling of the species being used, to the extent appropriate to their role.
(e) Responsibilities and activities of individuals assisting in a research project are consistent with their respective competencies.
(f) Psychologists make reasonable efforts to minimize the discomfort, infection, illness, and pain of animal subjects.
(g) A procedure subjecting animals to pain, stress, or privation is used only when an alternative procedure is unavailable and the goal is justified by its prospective scientific, educational, or applied value.
(h) Surgical procedures are performed under appropriate anesthesia; techniques to avoid infection and minimize pain are followed during and after surgery.
(i)When it is appropriate that the animal's life be terminated, it is done rapidly, with an effort to minimize pain, and in accordance with accepted procedures.

6.21 Reporting of Results.
(a) Psychologists do not fabricate data or falsify results in their publications.
(b) If psychologists discover significant errors in their published data, they take reasonable steps to correct such errors in a correction, retraction, erratum, or other appropriate publication means.

6.22 Plagiarism.
Psychologists do not present substantial portions or elements of another's work or data as their own, even if the other work or data source is cited occasionally.

6.23 Publication Credit.
(a) Psychologists take responsibility and credit, including authorship credit, only for work they have actually performed or to which they have contributed.
(b) Principal authorship and other publication credits accurately reflect the relative scientific or professional contributions of the individuals in-

volved, regardless of their relative status. Mere possession of an institutional position, such as Department Chair, does not justify authorship credit. Minor contributions to the research or to the writing for publications are appropriately acknowledged, such as in footnotes or in an introductory statement.

(c) A student is usually listed as principal author on any multiple-authored article that is substantially based on the student's dissertation or thesis.

6.24 Duplicate Publication of Data.

Psychologists do not publish, as original data, data that have been previously published. This does not preclude republishing data when they are accompanied by proper acknowledgment.

6.25 Sharing Data.

After research results are published, psychologists do not withhold the data on which their conclusions are based from other competent professionals who seek to verify the substantive claims through reanalysis and who intend to use such data only for that purpose, provided that the confidentiality of the participants can be protected and unless legal rights concerning proprietary data preclude their release.

6.26 Professional Reviewers.

Psychologists who review material submitted for publication, grant, or other research proposal review respect the confidentiality of and the proprietary rights in such information of those who submitted it.

7. FORENSIC ACTIVITIES

7.01 Professionalism.

Psychologists who perform forensic functions, such as assessments, interviews, consultations, reports, or expert testimony, must comply with all other provisions of this Ethics Code to the extent that they apply to such activities. In addition, psychologists base their forensic work on appropriate knowledge of and competence in the areas underlying such work, including specialized knowledge concerning special populations. (See also Standards 1.06, Basis for Scientific and Professional Judgments; 1.08, Human Differences; 1.15, Misuse of Psychologists' Influence; and 1.23, Documentation of Professional and Scientific Work.)

7.02 Forensic Assessments.

(a) Psychologists' forensic assessments, recommendations, and reports are based on information and techniques (including personal interviews of the individual, when appropriate) sufficient to provide appropriate substantiation for their findings. (See also Standards 1.03, Professional and Scientific Relationship; 1.23, Documentation of Professional and Scientific Work; 2.01, Evaluation, Diagnosis, and Interventions in Professional Context; and 2.05, Interpreting Assessment Results.)

(b) Except as noted in (c), below, psychologists provide written or oral forensic reports or testimony of the psychological characteristics of an individual only after they have conducted an examination of the individual adequate to support their statements or conclusions.

(c) When, despite reasonable efforts, such an examination is not feasible, psychologists clarify the impact of their limited information on the reliability and validity of their reports and testimony, and they appropriately limit the nature and extent of their conclusions or recommendations.

7.03 Clarification of Role.

In most circumstances, psychologists avoid performing multiple and potentially conflicting roles in forensic matters. When psychologists may be called on to serve in more than one role in a legal proceeding—for example, as consultant or expert for one party or for the court and as a fact witness—they clarify role expectations and the extent of confidentiality in advance to the extent feasible, and thereafter as changes occur, in order to avoid compromising their professional judgment and objectivity and in order to avoid misleading others regarding their role.

7.04 Truthfulness and Candor.

(a) In forensic testimony and reports, psychologists testify truthfully, honestly, and candidly and, consistent with applicable legal procedures, describe fairly the bases for their testimony and conclusions.

(b) Whenever necessary to avoid misleading, psychologists acknowledge the limits of their data or conclusions.

7.05 Prior Relationships.

A prior professional relationship with a party does not preclude psychologists from testifying as fact witnesses or from testifying to their services to the extent permitted by applicable law. Psychologists appropriately take into account ways in which the prior relationship might affect their professional objectivity or opinions and disclose the potential conflict to the relevant parties.

7.06 Compliance With Law and Rules.

In performing forensic roles, psychologists are reasonably familiar with the rules governing their roles. Psychologists are aware of the occasionally competing demands placed upon them by these principles and the requirements of the court system, and attempt to resolve these conflicts by making known their commitment to this Ethics Code and taking steps to resolve the conflict in a responsible manner. (See also Standard 1.02, Relationship of Ethics and Law.)

8. RESOLVING ETHICAL ISSUES

8.01 Familiarity With Ethics Code.

Psychologists have an obligation to be familiar with this Ethics Code, other applicable ethics codes, and their application to psychologists' work. Lack of awareness or misunderstanding of an ethical standard is not itself a defense to a charge of unethical conduct.

8.02 Confronting Ethical Issues.
When a psychologist is uncertain whether a particular situation or course of action would violate this Ethics Code, the psychologist ordinarily consults with other psychologists knowledgeable about ethical issues, with state or national psychology ethics committees, or with other appropriate authorities in order to choose a proper response.

8.03 Conflicts Between Ethics and Organizational Demands.
If the demands of an organization with which psychologists are affiliated conflict with this Ethics Code, psychologists clarify the nature of the conflict, make known their commitment to the Ethics Code, and to the extent feasible, seek to resolve the conflict in a way that permits the fullest adherence to the Ethics Code.

8.04 Informal Resolution of Ethical Violations.
When psychologists believe that there may have been an ethical violation by another psychologist, they attempt to resolve the issue by bringing it to the attention of that individual if an informal resolution appears appropriate and the intervention does not violate any confidentiality rights that may be involved.

8.05 Reporting Ethical Violations.
If an apparent ethical violation is not appropriate for informal resolution under Standard 8.04 or is not resolved properly in that fashion, psychologists take further action appropriate to the situation, unless such action conflicts with confidentiality rights in ways that cannot be resolved. Such action might include referral to state or national committees on professional ethics or to state licensing boards.

8.06 Cooperating With Ethics Committees.
Psychologists cooperate in ethics investigations, proceedings, and resulting requirements of the APA or any affiliated state psychological association to which they belong. In doing so, they make reasonable efforts to resolve any issues as to confidentiality. Failure to cooperate is itself an ethics violation.

8.07 Improper Complaints.
Psychologists do not file or encourage the filing of ethics complaints that are frivolous and are intended to harm the respondent rather than to protect the public.

Genograms

13

13.1 Definition

Psychologists who study family systems have found that the patterns of interactions among the members of our families significantly influence our emotions and the decisions we make in life. Would you like to gain a better understanding of the interactional patterns of your own family, and the ways in which these patterns have influenced you? If so, you may want to write a genogram paper. Also, if you are studying to become a psychologist, you may find the genogram to be a helpful diagnostic and therapeutic tool.

A genogram is a visual map of a family's relational, emotional, and biographical history. A completed genogram provides a summary of a family's history, which helps people understand complex and often vague patterns of family interaction. You may have always wondered, for example, why Aunt Sally went away for four years and no one ever answered your questions about her absence, or why your cousin Jane always seems to get more attention than you do at family gatherings. A genogram can help answer such questions.

Genograms have two parts. The first is a chart made up of symbols that represent at least three generations of your family members and the types of relationships among them. The second part of a genogram is a written story that explains the relationships among the people who are represented as symbols on the chart.

When you create a genogram you give yourself two views of your family. The first view is *vertical,* that is, multigenerational. This means that your genogram includes three generations:

1. You and your siblings
2. Your parents and their siblings
3. Your grandparents and their siblings.

At any of these levels, you can also add other important people such as a "nanny" or anyone who was considered part of the family.

The second view is *horizontal,* which means that you see what is going on within one generation, such as among your own brothers and sisters. You will write your genogram as if you were writing a story about your family. Storytelling and written histories have provided the tradition upon which the genogram is developed. Some families have well-developed traditions of storytelling that, at their best, entertain, teach, and guide. Your family story may have heroes and people who provided inspiration for you when you were growing up. At its worst, storytelling that demeans other family members can contribute to shame, misunderstanding, and alienation between members. If storytelling is not a conscious tradition in your family, chances are, with a little coaxing, you can remember many stories about your family.

Purpose

A genogram may change your life by increasing your understanding of yourself and of your family. Beyond the boundaries of your family, a genogram can help you understand how your neighborhood and the city or town in which it is located influenced your life. Because a genogram describes interactions among family members, it can illuminate your relationships with your girlfriend or boyfriend, as well as your relationships with employers and employees. For example, if you have a parent who was punitive, you are likely to perceive interactions with your teacher, coach, or employer as being potentially hurtful. In contrast, a nurturing relationship with a caregiver can often contribute to the formation of healthy adult relationships.

The purpose of this chapter is to show you how to use and understand the potential of the genogram. It will become an important tool should you go on to become a counselor or a psychologist and grow more adept at using the genogram therapeutically and interpretively. In medicine, a genogram provides a concise picture of the path of disease within a family. In psychotherapy, akin to its use in medicine, a genogram maps the history of adaptive and maladaptive patterns of behavior. Your vision and understanding of these patterns can be broadened and enhanced by the display of multigenerational history that your completed genogram provides.

Researchers have found that certain patterns of behavior and certain ways of thinking seem to be passed along from one generation to the next, often without much conscious awareness. By charting the members of your family back in time, starting with yourself and going back through three generations, and by using the tools and techniques that follow in this chapter, you will find new ways of understanding connections between a current situation, question, or problem and how that same situation evolved among your family members in other generations or settings. You may find new insights into how you think about problems or discover how much you resemble someone else in the family, such as the paternal grandmother you never knew. A genogram can give you a chance to decide if the past is indeed to be a prologue to the future.

13.2 How to Write a Genogram Paper

There are five basic steps in writing a genogram. Since each segment builds upon the previous one, you should follow the steps as outlined below:

1. List the members of your family.
2. Draw an initial diagram.
3. Write a narrative description of your diagram.
4. Add additional symbols and information to your diagram.
5. Interpret your diagram.

Step 1: List the Members of Your Family

This may seem simple at first glance, but some of you may have grown up in foster homes, with grandparents, in an orphanage, or with aunts or neighbors. The point is that you should include whomever you consider to be a member of your "family."

Two basic principles should guide your thinking about who to include in your family. First, include those people who are in true blood relationship to you. There may be cases where these people are not available to you. They may be dead, missing, or unknown to you due to adoptive circumstances, but include them anyway. Second, include those people who raised you, even if those people are not blood relatives. You may have more than one set of parents on your genogram. If you were adopted and know your biological parents as well as your adoptive parents, include them.

The following list attempts to enumerate all the possible people to include in your genogram:

- Yourself
- Brothers and sisters: Include natural, adopted, foster, step, half, and anyone else in your generation who might have lived with you, such as a cousin, an orphan your family took in, or an abandoned neighbor.
- Your parental generation: Include your biological parents, stepparents, foster parents, adoptive parents, and anyone else who acted in a parental role. If you grew up in a group home, for example, you may have related to someone in that setting as a parent (for example, clergy, house parent, or counselor).
- Your parents' siblings: Include your aunts and uncles—natural, step, adoptive, foster, and other. Add anyone else whom you called "aunt" or "uncle" but who were not blood relatives.

• Your grandparents' generation: Include your grandparents—natural, step, adoptive, foster, and other. Add anyone else you considered a grandparent who was not a blood relative.

Step 2: Draw an Initial Diagram

Draw your initial or first-draft diagram on a sheet of 8½-by-11-inch paper. You will eventually add additional information to this diagram in order to produce your final diagram, but your first diagram will include much of the most essential information.

Instead of drawing stick figures or caricatures of your family members, you will use symbols that represent them. The symbols used in genograms have evolved since Murray Bowen (1978) originated them in the late 1970s as a part of his pioneering work in family therapy. The symbols used in this text are adapted from those developed by the Task Force of the North American Primary Care Research Group, a group of family therapists and family physicians chaired by M. McGoldrick (McGoldrick & Gerson, 1985). The group attempted to create some standardization of symbols for a common language among therapists and physicians. Figure 13–1 provides most of the symbols you will you need to begin construction of the genogram.

Figure 13–2 is a sample diagram that illustrates how these basic symbols might be arranged to represent a hypothetical family we will call the Smiths. The author of the diagram, Lucy Smith, charted her brothers and sisters, parents, paternal grandparents, and a maternal grandmother and grandfather. Notice that the paternal line is usually on the left, the maternal line is usually on the right, and the oldest child is at the far left, with younger siblings on the right.

Now it is your turn. Take a piece of paper and draw your own diagram. Place the paper lengthwise as you work. About 2¼ inches from the bottom edge

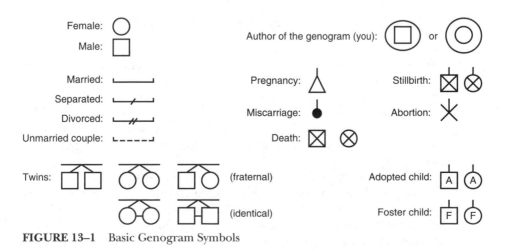

FIGURE 13–1   Basic Genogram Symbols

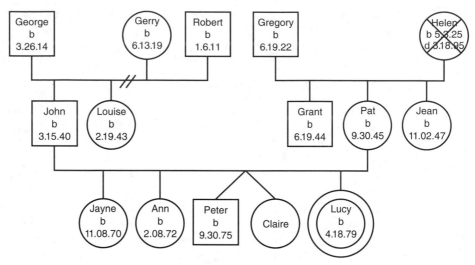

FIGURE 13–2   The Smith Family: Simple Initial Diagram

draw a horizontal line where you will put yourself and your siblings (see Figure 13–1). Allow about 2¼ inches for your parents' generation and another 2¼ inches for the grandparents. You may need to play around with the spacing on some scrap paper at first to get the symbols in reasonable balance with each other. The purpose of making the final chart tidy is to be able to write in figures and names and dates without making the genogram illegible. Spacing will also be a challenge in the cases of multiple stepparents.

After you have drawn the symbols for your family members, label yourself by name and age and do the same for any siblings placed on the same line as yourself. Now move up to your parents' generation, and then to grandparents, giving names and ages (see Figure 13–2).

Step 3: Write a Narrative Description of Your Diagram

Your next step is to write a story—a narrative description of your diagram. Tell the story of your life and your family by describing the people represented by the symbols on the diagram. Feel free to add additional symbols and other pertinent information to your diagram. Also, you will probably find that you are missing some important information, such as the date of birth or death of a relative. As you write, compile a list of the pieces of missing information so that you will be able to get this information when you have completed the initial draft of your narrative.

Begin your narrative by introducing yourself and, in a paragraph or so, telling your readers about the most important events in your life. For example, you might begin by saying, "I am 19 years old and the youngest of four children." Then continue by introducing and describing the members of your family. In addition to their names and ages, write such information as their places and dates of birth, their marital statuses with dates, and any children they might have (listed in birth order with gender and dates). If deaths in the family were the result of other-than-natural causes, indicate those causes. Add education levels, occupations, and religious or spiritual affiliations. Fill in as many of these details as you know now, while developing a list of questions to ask later. Suggestions for gathering data follow in another section. Continue your description with information about your siblings before moving on to your parents' and grandparents' generations. The challenge is to make the narrative flow as a story about several very interesting people. When you feel tempted just to list the details, recall the last time you read a boring piece of work, and be creative with your information!

As you write, add depth to your narrative by including details that begin to show the presence of any family patterns. Much in the same way that a jigsaw puzzle begins to make sense when enough of the pieces are in place, so family habits, preferences, or patterns may emerge as you develop your story. Include in your narrative anything that you think is meaningful. Consider including the following types of information to the extent that they are relevant to your family, but do not feel confined to these suggestions:

1. *Family relocation.* Did anyone in your family move to the United States from a foreign country? How often and at what ages did you move while growing up? How did moving affect extended family or other members within the family? For example, did moving bring on a clinical depression for Grandma? Was moving associated with job loss, loss of family members, better pay or living conditions?

2. *Health history.* What effect did ill or robust health have on your family? Include such conditions as alcoholism, eating disorders, mental or physical illness, and such activities as fitness exercises, and amateur or professional sports. How did family members respond to these conditions and activities? For instance, did they refuse to talk about health problems? Did they get outside or professional help? Did they leave the family or provide care?

3. *Incarcerations.* How do family members respond to the prison sentence of a relative? Do they move away from, socially withdraw from, ignore, or visit and support that person? Do they become social activists for prison reform?

4. *Family and community relationships.* How do family members get along day to day in their jobs and communities? Have you heard family stories about Auntie Charisse, who never missed a day of work in her life? Or what about Grandpa, who always played Santa Claus each year at the elementary school, and, who, until he died at 91, showed up at school each May Day to fly kites with the third graders? Perhaps your younger sister has trouble keeping a job for more than six months; how do you account for that and what does your family say? Does anyone else in the family have a similar problem? How do community members see your family members (e.g., are they thought of as hard working, fickle, upstanding, unreliable)?

At this point, your job is to write information about life among the members of your family using the forgoing as a guide. If there are unique qualities about your family, please add them. Try to be alert to coincidences and mindful of any repeating patterns of behavior, attitudes, or values.

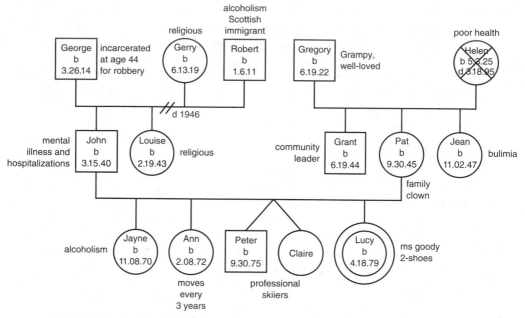

FIGURE 13–3   The Smith Family: Detailed Diagram

As you write, address the questions within one generation; then move on to those within the second and third generations. In other words, you will be describing how your family responds to major changes as well as garden-variety joys and disappointments. If a common theme is strong in your family, organize the story around how that theme operates across generations, and provide comparisons of one generation with the others. For example, you may notice that all the women in your family have unusual physical talents, starting with your maternal grandmother, who was a ballet dancer, your mother, who continued her downhill ski racing career into her late thirties, and your kid sister, who is the Northeastern billiards champion in the under-20-year-old division. The point here is to explore the commonalties and differences within the generations of your family.

Step 4: Add Additional Symbols and Information to Your Diagram

In your paper, you can indicate six qualities of relationship between people represented on the diagram: close, very close, conflict, irritated affection, distance, and cutoff. A *close relationship* exists between people who like each other and are caring and supportive. A *very close relationship* is characterized by such overinvolvement between two family members that neither one has a clear and separate identity. A *conflict* happens when someone is not getting along well with another family member. Most observers can experience the tension between these two family members while in their presence. There is disagreement, discomfort, and dislike. I might add here that the conflict could be between, say, your parent and a former spouse, even though they are no longer in the same household.

An *irritated affection* describes disagreement, agitation, and discomfort between two people, but without the element of disliking each other. This kind of relationship has a contentious quality of bickering and arguing that masks unexpressed affection. In contrast, the quality of *distance* in a family relationship reflects the desire of one member to avoid contact with another out of apathy rather than a need to conceal affection. Finally, a *cutoff* is a term coined to describe an abrupt break with another family member. Unlike an apathetic, distance-type relationship, a cutoff is decisive and often negatively charged so far as emotions are concerned. A person may have very strong feelings for another yet will deny any resolution of those feelings by running away or claiming no connection. For example, is there anyone in your family who has moved far away and refuses to return? Is there still a charged emotional connection evident whenever this person's name comes up (Marlin, 1989; McGoldrick & Gerson, 1985)?

Using Figure 13–4 as a model, add these symbols to your existing diagram according to your perceptions of familial relationships.

By looking at the strength and nature of relationships, it is easy to see how disconnected or connected the family is. Unlike the objective, factual information of Step 1 or the details of Step 3, emotional distance is a more subjective assessment. By graphically mapping these qualities of relating, the genogram at this stage (see Figure 13–5) facilitates a view of how family patterns replicate themselves across many generations, thereby providing you with the perspective you need to make some interpretations.

We mentioned before that as you write you may find that you do not have some necessary pieces of information. As a member of your family, you have the most direct access to the information you want. However, that access is not always as easy as it might seem. You might be reluctant to ask for what you want due to things you have learned about your family by growing up in it, like knowing never to ask Dad about the war years or not talking to Mom about her first marriage. These secret areas are often the very ones you are doing a genogram about in the first place, because they represent gaps in your understanding of your family and your place in the family.

This is as good a place as any to alert you to some pitfalls you may encounter while writing a genogram. Asking questions may require care and con-

FIGURE 13–4   Relationship Symbols

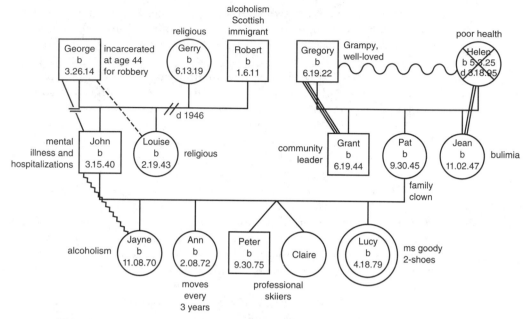

FIGURE 13–5   The Smith Family: Final Diagram

sideration. For example, a colleague working on a genogram shared the following concern: "Asking questions could be awful! My mother's father was executed in a Russian prison camp. Bringing it up would make her go to pieces." When you know an issue is sensitive, use wisdom to guide your inquiry. However, you may stumble into an issue that catches you by surprise because you knew nothing about it. If you inadvertently create a problem, ask other members of your family to help you. My colleague may have needed to calm down her mother, remaining with her for a while and asking others to help keep an eye on her. If you are uneasy with a face-to-face meeting with a family member, here are a few alternative ideas. Write down the questions you want answered and mail them to the relative. Have the person tape record the replies and send you the tape. Another idea may be to ask your questions over the phone.

Choose a good time to broach the subject with parents or siblings. Explain that you have a class assignment and need their help. Depending on the climate in your family, you might tell them you are trying to understand some aspects of yourself or of your own behavior. Ask permission to ask them questions and to tape record their answers. Getting the information you want is sometimes a challenge that requires persistence and creativity on your part. For example, I had the idea my family was quite open to talking, but I ran into uncharacteristic silence from my mother when I asked about bad crop years on the potato farm while she was growing up. My grandmother, too, was happy to sit with me and talk about her childhood—until I turned on the tape recorder! She required reassurance about the private nature of the recording, and she needed help in getting used to the sound of her recorded voice. I suspect you, too, will figure out what you need to do in your family to find information.

Some family members may not always be eager to talk to you about themselves. It is important to approach them with respect and accept a "No, thank you" if that is their wish at the time. Don't be afraid to ask on another occasion, however. Talking about family business can threaten to expose private fears or trigger a desire to protect someone. If your requests to talk are rejected by some family members, go on to others, perhaps siblings or cousins. At times and with certain issues, the further away from the "heart" of the family, the easier it is for members to talk.

Often, by interviewing various members of the family, you begin to perceive a different picture from the one you held. Perhaps you can think of an example right now of two relatives who have a totally different view of a third relative. Relationship to the person of inquiry, age differences, and intergenerational effects add to the challenge of sorting out the new information you get and the challenge of writing the information down clearly.

Friends are a good source to bring balance to the myopic view you can develop of your own family. Friends can help to temper outrageous family reactions, and friends can also point out rough places to which some family members are blind. Family Bibles or other documents are great sources of information about details such as names, dates, marriages, births, and deaths, though they provide little in the way of information about the quality of a relationship or its strength. Newspaper articles about your family or a member of the family can be insightful. Personal diaries (read with permission!), essays, stories, even artwork can be a window to thoughts.

Step 5: Interpret Your Diagram

The purpose of this step is for you to make sense for yourself of what you have learned about your family and write it down. The task is interpretive and, as it is your own perception of how things are, your brothers or sisters may not agree with what you write. As you interpret your diagram, consider the following questions.

- What kinds of relationships exist between you and any of your siblings, between you and either (or any) of your parents? Between you and grandparents? What relationships do you observe among other family members?

- Are there any "triangles"? Just suppose that your younger brother is very close to your mother and in conflict with your father. Connect the relationship between mother and father to create a *graphic triangle*. What do you observe about that relationship, and what effect does it have on you or another family member?

- Have you discovered any family myths? Who knows about the myths and who does not? Are there tendencies for certain people to be rescuers, fighters, peacemakers? Are the myths retold at family gatherings, cocktail parties, on the golf course, at pubs, with men only or women only? Are there any themes to the family myths?

- Have you discovered any secrets? Who else knows, and who does not know? Here's an example: A client once shared with me her amazement at finding out as a young adult that her mother was an alcoholic. For years the client thought her mother was "in a funny mood" or "crazy." The secret was so secure that the family did not inform her earlier. Does information travel a predictable path through your family? In other words, does your mother first tell news, say, to your older sister, who tells her middle son, who then tells you?
- Is birth order important in your family? Are first-born children in each generation treated similarly? Do they act similarly? Are terms such as "Son" or "Junior" or "Baby" used with certain children? Is a pattern revealed in which a particular birth-order child seems to receive special attention, positive or negative? Is anyone left out of the loop? Are there several husbands or wives with the same name? Same jobs?
- Are there any cutoff roots? What are your observations of family members who don't speak to each other? Have family members moved away and not been seen again? What words are used by the family to describe these relatives or the situations surrounding their move away from the family?

The final paragraph of your paper should summarize the insights you have gained and the conclusions that you have drawn about the relationships in your family and how they affect you.

The Components of a Genogram Paper

A genogram paper has these components:

1. Title page
2. Body of the paper, which includes:
   a. A narrative that describes the people and relationships indicated on your genogram
   b. A narrative that interprets the relationships indicated in the genogram
3. Appendix, consisting of your final family diagram (genogram), to which you refer in writing your paper

13.3 Postscript: Additional Applications for Genograms

Genograms have a number of applications in addition to the ones discussed above. For example, because a genogram can be developed from a simple chart of family members and shared with others in a group, a genogram can be a focus for group therapy or a support group project. For more depth, the genogram can identify family traditions or habits that have been obscured by the clutter of everyday business. Coincidences can be instructive for modifying ideas about the path family members must take in career or marriage. For example, it might be helpful to have an understanding that most of the women on your mother's side have married school teachers. That awareness can be particularly helpful when trying to understand the family's disdain for your marriage plans with an aeronautical engineer.

Another purpose for doing a genogram could be to solve a specific problem. At important decision-making times, a genogram could clarify trouble areas and lead to more illuminated choices. For example, suppose you are unhappy in your job and are planning to change careers. It can be helpful to look into the family picture and find out who else made changes in career direction and why. You can ask the ones still living about themselves and also what they remember about those family members you did not know.

References

Agassiz, L. (1958). *A scientist of two worlds: Louis Agassiz* (C.O. Pearce, Ed.) Philadelphia: Lippincott.

American Psychiatric Association. (1994). *Diagnostic and statistical manual of mental disorders* (4th ed.). Washington, DC: Author.

American Psychological Association. (1992). *Ethical principles of psychologists and code of conduct.* Washington, DC: Author.

American Psychological Association. (1994). *Publication manual of the American Psychological Association* (4th ed.). Washington, DC: Author.

Bowen, M. (1978). *Family therapy in clinical practice.* New York: Jason Aronson.

Brundage, D., Keane, R., & Mackneson, R. (1993). Application of learning theory to the instruction of adults. In Thelma Barer-Stein & James A. Draper (Eds.), *The craft of teaching adults* (pp. 131–144). Toronto, Ontario: Culture Concepts.

Carr, Sarah. (2000, March 10). Online psychology instruction is effective, but not satisfying, study finds. *The Chronicle of Higher Education* [On-line serial]. Available: http://chronicle.com/weekly/v46/i27/27a04801.htm.

Clay, R. A. (1997). Research reveals the health benefits of pet ownership. *APA Monitor, 28*(8), 14–15.

Cogar, M. M., & Hill, C. E. (1992). Examining the effects of brief individual dream interpretation. *Dreaming, 2,* 239–248.

Diemer, R., Lobell, L., Vivino, B., & Hill, C. E. (1996). A comparison of dream interpretation, event interpretation, and unstructured session in brief therapy. *Journal of Counseling Psychology, 43,* 99–112.

Falk, D. R., & Hill, C. E. (1995). The effectiveness of dream interpretation groups for women in a divorce transition. *Dreaming, 5,* 29–42.

Fromm, E. (1964). *The heart of man: Its genius for good and evil.* New York: Bantam Books.

Fromm, E. (1967). *Psychoanalysis and religion.* New York: Bantam Books.

Hartwell, P. (1985). Grammar, grammars, and the teaching of grammar. *College English, 47,* 105–127.

Hill, C. E., Diemer, R. A., & Heaton, K. J. (1997). Dream interpretation sessions: Who volunteers, who benefits, and what volunteer clients view as most and least helpful. *Journal of Counseling Psychology, 44,* 53–62.

Humphreys, K. (1996). Clinical psychologists as psychotherapists: History, future, and alternatives. *American Psychologist, 51*(3), 190–197.

Larson, R. W. (2000). Toward a psychology of positive youth development. *American Psychologist, 55*(1), 170–183.

Li, X., & Crane, N. B. (1993). *Electronic style: A guide to citing electronic information.* Westport, CT: Meckler.

Lochner, B. T., & Melchert, T. P. (1997). Relationship of cognitive style and theoretical orientation to psychology interns' preferences for supervision. *Journal of Counseling Psychology, 44,* 256–260.

Lucas, M. (1997). Identity development, career development, and psychological separation from parents: Similarities and differences between men and women. *Journal of Counseling Psychology, 44,* 123–132.

Lunsford, A., & Connors, R. (1992). *The St. Martin's handbook* (2nd ed. [Annotated instructor's ed.]). New York: St. Martin's.

Marlin, E. (1989). *Genograms.* Lincolnwood, IL: NTC/Contemporary Publishing.

May, R. (1975). *The courage to create.* New York: Norton.

McGoldrick, M. & Gerson, R. (1985). *Genograms in family assessment.* New York: W. W. Norton.

Morgan, A. (1991). *Research into student learning in distance education.* Vicotria, Australia: University of South Australia, Underdale.

Parry, A., & Doan, R. (1994). *Story re-visions: Narrative therapy in the postmodern world.* New York: The Guilford Press.

Pearce, C. O. (Ed.). (1958). *A scientist of two worlds: Louis Agassiz.* Philadelphia: Lippincott.

Pinkola-Estes, C. (1992). *Women who run with the wolves.* New York: Ballantine Books.

Rainey, L. M., & Borders, L. D. (1997). Influential factors in career orientation and career aspirations of early adolescent girls. *Journal of Counseling Psychology, 44,* 160–172.

Richie, B. S., Fassinger, R. E., Linn, S. G., Johnson, J., Prosser, J., & Robinson, S. (1997). Persistence, connection, and passion: A qualitative study of the career development of highly achieving African American-Black and White Women. *Journal of Counseling Psychology, 44,* 133–148.

Rosenthal, R., & Rosnow, R. L. (1996). *The volunteer subject.* New York: Wiley.

Schuchman, M., Weber, N., & Shaw, T. (1997). *Effects of attractiveness on social acceptance of therapy patients.* Unpublished manuscript, University of Central Oklahoma.

Shaughnessy, M. (1977). *Errors and expectations: A guide for the teacher of basic writing.* New York: Oxford University Press.

U.S. Department of Eudcation. (1999). National Center For Education Statistics Statistical Analysis. *Distance Education at Postsecondary Education Institutions Report December 1999.*

Index